1992

REFUGEES AND
THE ASYLUM DILEMMA
IN THE WEST

Issues in Policy History
General Editor: Donald T. Critchlow

REFUGEES AND THE ASYLUM DILEMMA IN THE WEST

Edited by
Gil Loescher

The Pennsylvania State University Press
University Park, Pennsylvania

This work was originally published as a special issue of *Journal of Policy History* (vol. 4, no. 1, 1992). This is its first separate paperback publication.

Library of Congress Cataloging-in-Publication Data

Refugees and the asylum dilemma in the West / edited by Gil Loescher.

    p.   cm.
Includes bibliographical references.
ISBN 0-271-00856-3
  1. Refugees—Legal status, laws, etc.—Europe. 2. Asylum, Right of—Europe. 3. Refugees—Legal status, laws, etc.—North America.
4. Asylum, Right of—North America. I. Loescher, Gil.
K3230.R45R443   1992
342.4′083—dc20
[344.0283]   91–45375
                                                    CIP

Contents

Editor's Preface

The collapse of the Soviet Union and the changing political order in Southeast Asia and Central America have created an asylum and refugee problem of such immense proportion as to qualify any sense of euphoria produced by the new world order. Even the former Communist regimes of Poland and Hungary confronted seemingly insurmountable problems from the army of refugees that fled west from Romania, Albania, and the east. While West Germany experienced its own outbreak of xenophobia and anti-immigrant hatred, officials in Warsaw heard a public outcry from their own citizens concerning the refugee camps of Romanians and Ukrainians that had sprung up throughout the city. The refugee problem, as it appeared in Europe, showed in all too dramatic a fashion that indeed the walls dividing East and West had been torn down.

This volume, edited by Gil Loescher, examines the contemporary refugee and asylum problem within a historical framework. These essays suggest that refugee policies established in the past will no longer serve the present. The historical lesson in this case might well be that history offers us little in the way of a specific prescription for the future. Many of the past policies, as they developed in the United States, Canada, and Western Europe, emerged as responses to the refugee problems created by the rise of fascism in interwar Europe, the end of World War II, and competition between the East and West during Cold War years. Although the Western democracies committed themselves, as Loescher observes, to "the creation of an international refugee regime," refugee policy still tended to remain restrictive.

Recent problems have led Western governments to introduce new measures to limit further the number of refugees entering their countries. Limitations have been placed on visas, while asylum-seekers at ports of entry have been placed in detention centers or repatriated to their home countries. Only in rare cases—largely due to political pressures within the host country—have exceptions been made, as in the case of Cubans in the United States or the recent case of homosexuals in Canada.

These essays argue forcefully that restrictive measures will only further exacerbate domestic problems with the Western democracies and threaten economic and social stability in those countries experiencing political change.

This volume provides students, scholars, and policymakers with a concise examination of the historical context and present implications of the refugee and asylum problem that faces us today. This volume presents an opportunity to engage in a profound discussion of a crucial question that will shape the course of history in our time.

Donald T. Critchlow
General Editor

GIL LOESCHER

Refugees and the Asylum Dilemma in the West

In recent years, political asylum and refugees have become acute issues in public debate in Western Europe and North America. The debate has become especially heated since 1989 and the breaching of barriers between Eastern and Western Europe, with East Germans, Albanians, Romanians, and Yugoslavs all trying to move west. Most asylum-seekers continue to come from the Third World. Those who manage to enter the West face growing hostility, poverty, and even violent attacks. In France immigration has already shifted political discourse sharply to the right, testing the nation's tolerance toward foreigners and shaking its liberal foundations. Xenophobia and brutal physical attacks on foreigners by skinheads and extreme right-wingers throughout Germany have caused politicians in Bonn to reconsider their country's asylum provisions. Governments everywhere appear reluctant to open their doors when they are not sure how many will benefit from their hospitality and for how long. To many industrialized countries, asylum-seekers are perceived mostly as economic migrants in search of a better life. Actual migratory pressures from the South and perceived threats of exodus from the East have only served to reinforce this restrictive attitude to asylum. The refugee problem has reached such a critical point that the very institution of asylum is being threatened.

Migration Pressures on Asylum Systems

It is only recently that Western governments ever envisaged a large-scale movement of the poor from countries northward to Western Europe and

JOURNAL OF POLICY HISTORY, Vol. 4, No. 1, 1992.

North America. The 1980s and 1990s have rudely shaken the industrialized countries out of their old notions. Today's refugees are only part of the millions caught up in the crosscurrents of ethnic and civil wars, famine and poverty, who have been forced into exile. Most of these new arrivals do not fit the image of refugees for whom most Westerners have had ready sympathy in the past. Asylum-seekers today generally have few political and cultural links with the industrialized countries; their religions are foreign and their ways of life completely alien. Refugees are seen by many in the West as a threat to their way of life.

The unexpected arrival in the West of large numbers of people with a variety of claims to asylum has severely jolted existing practices and has overtaxed the procedural systems for handling refugee determinations. Once in the West, the majority of asylum-seekers stay, sometimes for several years, working through appeal procedures up to and including judicial review. In Germany, for example, despite the introduction of accelerated procedures for some applicants, it can take many years for a final determination to be made. In other countries it takes eighteen months or longer. The substantial backlog of claims results in claimants remaining even longer in Western countries and requiring additional material assistance, thus putting a considerable strain on reception and integration facilities.

The reality is that the present increase in the number of asylum-seekers and refugees is neither a temporary phenomenon nor a random product of chance events. Rather, it is the predictable consequence of fundamental political, demographic, economic, and ecological crises occurring throughout the Third World and Eastern Europe. Although the Cold War and East-West competition in the developing world had been responsible for most refugee movements in the past, the collapse of Communism in large parts of the world has not diminished the risks of displacement. The number of refugees and migrants are on the rise all over the world. Indeed, there are fears that many more could become displaced in the future as nationalistic, ethnic, and religious tensions, previously suppressed by totalitarian regimes and by East-West conflict, are now unleashed, potentially leading to violence.

Building Walls in the West

Governments act as though the most effective way to limit asylum-seekers is to prevent them from arriving in the first place. In recent years the West has been building barriers by adopting restrictive practices and deterrent measures to curb new arrivals. For the past several years nearly all Western governments have introduced measures to make access more difficult and to limit the number of asylum claims within their judicial systems. Some governments, particularly in Western Europe, have severely limited the rights of asylum-seekers to housing, employment, social welfare benefits, language training, and counseling and advice services. Nearly all Western states are systematically enforcing strict limitations on the ability of refugees to seek out a place of asylum by imposing visas, fining airline and shipping companies for carrying "undocumented aliens," refusing entry, locking up some asylum-seekers at ports of entry and in detention centers, and putting other restrictions on movement.

Government officials believe that the deterrents will lead to fewer applicants, thus reducing the xenophobic, racial, and political tensions arising from the unregulated arrival of unwanted foreigners. The result of such measures is that now asylum is not only difficult to obtain, but it is becoming increasingly difficult even to reach a point at which an application can be made.

The Limitations of Restrictionism

Despite deterrent measures, the number of asylum applications in the West rose from 95,000 in 1983 to about 548,000 in 1990. Not only does deterrence not seem to work, but it has serious repercussions for genuine refugees and undermines the entire international regime. Restrictive measures fall indiscriminately and with equal weight on illegal aliens and "bona fide" refugees. Detention, crowded and austere living conditions, and the total lack of opportunity for employment must be endured by refugee and illegal alien alike. Many are isolated and deprived of any reorientation and adjustment to a new environment. In most Western countries, where it can take months or even years to process asylum claims, by the time asylum-seekers are recognized as refugees, many have been rendered totally unfit for integration into their new societies.

Simply building new barriers around Western countries will not make the refugee problem go away. Restrictive measures taken unilaterally by Western states serve not to solve the problem but to pass it on to some other country to resolve, thus contributing to interstate tensions, protectionism, and a breakdown in the international refugee regime.

The objective of this volume is to examine the historical background and contemporary significance of the asylum and refugee issue confronting

Western governments and to draw lessons for policy-making in this area in the future. Past studies of the asylum problem have focused narrowly on the conditions in receiving countries and have failed to see the global interconnectedness of the refugee problem. This volume is unique in that it examines not only the history of policies of receiving nations in the West but also some of the underlying causes of refugee movements. The authors also argue that to really resolve the asylum problem in the West policymakers must direct their attention toward the conditions outside the industrialized countries that cause mass movements of populations, as well as toward the improvement of their own asylum procedures.

Claudena Skran considers the current asylum dilemma in the West by examining refugee movements and national responses to them in a historical perspective. She argues that mass refugee movements and asylum crises have been an important international political issue throughout most of this century. Seventy years ago Western governments committed themselves to the creation of an international refugee regime, recognizing that to do otherwise would be detrimental to regional and international stability. Yet the refugee crises of the interwar period and the Holocaust demonstrate that the development of immigration restrictions worldwide made solutions to refugee problems extremely difficult. The danger exists today that the international community may be in the process of re-creating a situation reminiscent of that of dispossessed Jews in the 1930s, where large numbers of unwanted people were barred from entry to any place where they might be able to reestablish themselves.

As the industrialized nations build a fortress to keep out asylum-seekers and migrants, those same nations are failing to address the root causes of the exodus—widespread human rights abuse, arms sales to areas of tension, and the burden of debt on the Third World. Mark Gibney examines the international political context in which refugee flows occur. In recent years internal strife and East-West conflict in the Third World have been responsible for most major refugee movements. Unfortunately, even though many regional conflicts appear to be moving toward peaceful resolution, a return home for many refugees is either not feasible or is extremely difficult. Most of the countries to which refugees are returning or will return have been devastated by years, and sometimes decades, of war. They already have large numbers of internally displaced people and little or no capacity to reintegrate those who left. Entire villages have been leveled; irrigation systems and other infrastructure have been destroyed; people have lost their homes and land; the economy has been brought to a virtual standstill; and vast amounts of territory have been mined. Given the depth and duration of these problems and the responsibility of the superpowers for fueling these conflicts in the past, it will be difficult for these countries to pull themselves out of their current crises without considerable international assistance. Gibney argues that refugee movements are frequently one of the major unintended consequences of foreign-policy interventions that have been initiated for altogether different purposes and which last long beyond the intervention itself. While this observation has been made before, it is well worth restating, as foreign policy, particularly U.S. foreign policy, continues to be made and executed with virtually no regard for its migration and immigration ramifications. Given the migration and refugee pressures confronting the world today, the virtual exclusion of any consideration of the migratory effects of strategic and foreign policies has got to change if we are to make any progress toward resolving the global refugee problem.

During most of the past decade, the asylum system in the United States was deadlocked in a confrontation between government agencies seemingly determined to limit the numbers of refugees entering the country and refugee advocates, including lawyers and civil rights groups, endeavoring to secure the minimum rights contained in U.S. refugee law. Norman and Naomi Flink Zucker trace the history of American policy, focusing in particular on the post–World War II period, when U.S. legislation defined a refugee primarily as someone who was escaping from a Communist country. Although the Refugee Act of 1980 removed these ideological restrictions, the United States continued throughout the decade to use asylum and refugee policy as a foreign-policy instrument. With the beginning of the 1990s, however, several important developments have raised hopes that U.S. asylum policy might become more evenhanded and responsive in the future. The attorney general issued new asylum regulations in 1991 that are intended to make the asylum process fairer and more consistent. The adjudication process has been removed from the enforcement division of the Immigration and Naturalization Service and placed in an independent agency staffed with specially trained asylum officers familiar with human rights law and political conditions in countries of origin. In this way, it is hoped that foreign-policy concerns will no longer exert a major influence on asylum decisions.

Canada's historical response to refugees and asylum-seekers has been remarkably similar to that of its southern neighbor. James Hathaway notes that Canada traditionally was a country of immigration and only recently has become a country of first asylum. Like the United States, Canada participated actively in the drafting of the 1951 Convention relating to the Status of Refugees but did not sign the accord. During most of the Cold War, Canada admitted refugees who either served the country's economic or political interests and mostly constituted people fleeing Eastern European regimes. In the 1970s Canada implemented refugee legislation (preceding the United States by several years), but the asylum system came under serious pressure in the 1980s as increasingly larger numbers of asylum claims were made. This precipitated a series of reforms that culminated in 1989 when the government established the Convention Refugee Determination Division of the Immigration and Refugee Board, which is the sole authority charged with the protection of refugees in Canada. To support the activities of the board and to ensure informed and impartial decision-making on asylum cases, a Documentation Center with extensive information on human rights conditions in countries of origin was also established. After two years in operation, it is generally acknowledged that compared to the asylum systems in Western Europe and elsewhere, Canada's procedures are currently among the fairest and most open in the West.

Perhaps the region most in need of change is Western Europe, where a regionwide effort to stem the influx of asylum-seekers is currently under way. Philip Rudge documents not only the racism and xenophobia that have always been a part of European society but also the relatively liberal asylum and immigration policies that characterized the early Cold War period in Europe. Europe-wide cooperation on asylum has greatly increased after the decision by European Community heads of state to create a "Single Europe" by 1993. In December 1988 an intergovernmental group of coordinators was established to formulate plans for dealing with asylum-seekers in 1993. A program was drawn up that included two conventions. The first, approved at the Dublin summit of EC heads of state in June 1990, identified procedures for determining the state responsible for examining an asylum request. The second dealt with procedures for crossing the future external border of the European Community, including provisions on visas and sanctions against transport companies, and was ratified in mid-1991. Parallel with these EC initiatives, the five countries at the center of Europe—Germany, France, and the Benelux countries—signed the Schengen agreement, which contains provisions for uniform principles in controlling their common borders, for the harmonization of conditions of entry and visa requirements, and also includes agreement on the determination of the country responsible for receiving an asylum request. In addition, a permanent information system known as the Schengen Information System will be set up and computerized, listing the personal details of all asylum-seekers. It is likely that other EC states will join the Schengen agreement. Italy, Spain, and Portugal have already become parties to the agreement.

The concern on the part of Rudge and others is whether European governments can successfully reconcile the right of refugees to a fair determination of their claims to asylum with the need to maintain an effective immigrant control mechanism. The way the European Community resolves this policy dilemma concerns not only the fate of asylum-seekers in Western Europe but will undoubtedly affect the asylum policies of the rest of the industrialized world as well.

The Need to Address the Underlying Causes

The one certain lesson we can draw from the past is that building walls is no answer against those who feel compelled to move. The only effective way of dealing with the problem is to address the conditions that create refugees and migrants. To do so, the problems of asylum and migration need to be taken as seriously as other major problems in foreign or strategic policy. Governments need to develop policies that will give greater priority to political and economic reform in the countries of emigration, providing adequate levels of assistance, investment, and openness in trade to promote effective development in the Third World and Eastern Europe. A failure to take action to stem poverty, violence, persecution, and other factors that generate migration will have direct or indirect repercussions for the security of the industrialized world itself. In the future, policymakers must factor the problems and issues raised by mass international migrations into calculations on foreign and security policy.

CLAUDENA M. SKRAN

The International Refugee Regime: The Historical and Contemporary Context of International Responses to Asylum Problems

In the 1990s, an increasing number of refugees make their way to the countries of the West. While the annual number of asylum seekers to Western Europe and North America averaged about 20,000 in the mid-1970s, by 1990 this figure had jumped to more than 500,000.[1] Unlike previous migrants, many of these asylum seekers came from non-Western countries, including Iran, Turkey, Sri Lanka, and Ghana.[2] Their flight to the West was but a small part of a worldwide refugee problem that has grown larger since the 1980s, especially in the Third World. The vast majority of the 17.5 million people now considered to be refugees are located in Asia, Africa, and Latin America. Despite the improved international climate created by the thaw of the Cold War, the current asylum crisis is likely to continue throughout the decade; the mass exodus of Kurds to Turkey and Iran in the aftermath of the Persian Gulf war is one reminder of this.

In response to increasing arrivals in the West, many traditional countries of asylum have adopted harsher policies toward refugees. According to human rights adovcates, these policies contradict the humanitarian traditions of the West.[3] Moreover, they threaten the foundation of the international refugee regime established to deal with refugees after World War II, a regime that Western countries were instrumental in creating. These developments bring into question the ability of international institutions, accustomed to resettling small numbers of dissidents from Eastern Europe and carrying out refugee relief in the Third World, to adequately deal with refugee issues today. Consequently, the international refugee regime is at an important crossroads. Can the institutions originally forged in the Cold War era be adapted to meet current and future asylum prob-

JOURNAL OF POLICY HISTORY, Vol. 4, No. 1, 1992.

lems? This article attempts to place this question in historical perspective by considering refugee movements and international responses to them since World War I. In considering these issues, we can draw on a more than seventy-year history of organized assistance to refugees.

The Nature of Refugee Movements and Asylum Problems

There is a common tendency to think of refugees as a relatively new issue that primarily affects Third World countries. William Smyser, for instance, has written that "the second half of the twentieth century has been witness to an unprecedented explosion in the number and impact of refugees."[4] While it is true that most refugees since 1945 have fled violent conflicts or persecution in the developing world, they are neither new nor exclusive to the Third World. Instead, they have been an enduring and global issue throughout this century. These refugee movements began in the early twentieth century, when the Balkan wars forced several hundred thousand people to flee their home countries.[5] The two world wars uprooted even more. World War II alone displaced a staggering number of people—more than thirty million. Even during the relatively peaceful interwar period, at least seven million people became refugees, including Germans, Poles, Hungarians, Russians, Greeks, Turks, Armenians, Bulgarians, Spaniards, and Jews.[6]

Throughout the Cold War, the European continent continued to produce refugees, primarily individuals fleeing communist regimes in the Soviet Union and its satellites in Eastern Europe. During the same period, mass refugee movements came to characterize the developing world. Anticolonial struggles or violent conflicts in newly created states uprooted thousands in Africa and Asia in the 1960s and 1970s.[7] In the 1980s political and environmental castastrophes combined to produce some of the largest refugee groups since World War II. The Soviet invasion of Afghanistan, for instance, forced more than five million Afghan refugees into Pakistan and Iran. In the Horn of Africa, civil war and famine provoked a mass exodus of more than one million people. In Central America, civil wars in Nicaragua, El Salvador, and Guatemala drove almost 300,000 people to seek asylum outside their borders and displaced more than one million internally.[8]

It is highly unlikely that refugees will disappear from the agenda of international politics in the near future. The end of the Cold War in Europe has unleashed political and ethnic conflicts that encourage forced migration. In 1989 loosened border restrictions enabled an estimated 1.2

million people, including ethnic Germans, Bulgarian Turks, Soviet Jews, and Poles, to move from Eastern to Western Europe. Soviet plans to eliminate all travel restriction could produce 2 to 2.5 million emigrants annually.[9] If internal conflict within Soviet republics leads to chaos, a mass exodus from and within the former Soviet Union looms as a possibility. Violent clashes between Azerbaijanis and Armenians have already uprooted 400,000.[10] Ethnic conflict and political uncertainty in Romania, Albania, Yugoslavia, and Bulgaria and elsewhere in Eastern Europe also threaten to produce both external and internal refugees in the 1990s. In the Third World, the continuation of civil conflicts, economic deprivation, and population pressures make it likely that mass migrations will continue for the foreseeable future. In addition, the devastating impact of deforestation, desertification, and global warming may add an entirely new category of refugees: an estimated ten million "environmental refugees" have already been forced to leave their homes, and their ranks will swell if environmental degradation continues unabated.[11]

The Causes and Consequences of Refugee Movements

Despite the differing locations of refugee movements before and after 1945, common causes of refugee movements can be identified. In the words of Sir John Hope Simpson, director of the refugee survey conducted by the Royal Institute for International Affairs in the late 1930s, "The cause of every refugee movement is tyranny of one kind or another, but the forms of tyranny differ."[12] In the nineteenth century, tyrannical governments produced refugees when suppressing challenges to their authority. Their activities, however, usually created only a small number of revolutionary exiles, leaving the majority of the population relatively unaffected. In contrast, political changes within a country in the twentieth century have often affected entire socieites. Add to this the incredible destructive capabilities available to governments using modern technology and one has a recipe for both genocide and mass exodus. For instance, in the interwar period the rise of totalitarian governments, including the National Socialists in Germany and the communists in the Soviet Union, produced millions of refugees.[13] In writing of the postwar era, Leon Gordenker points out that government brutality aimed at preventing social change has created refugee movements in Argentina, Guatemala, El Salvador, and Uganda.[14]

War and civil war have also been a persistent cause of refugee movements in the twentieth century. Although interstate war has always produced some refugees, it is only in the age of total war that international conflict has uprooted millions, as shown in and World Wars I and II.[15] In the developing world today, civil wars, or violent conflicts over the social order, are especially likely to create both internally and externally displaced people.[16] In this regard, foreign intervention in civil wars and the global proliferation of modern weapons technology have exacerbated conflicts fought in the Third World. In addition, rising levels of population density worldwide mean that it is increasingly likely that civilian populations will be affected in civil wars.[17] While economic underdevelopment by itself is not a major cause of refugee movements, it can contribute to social conflict within societies.[18] In some cases the impact of a war or civil war on refugee movements may be increased if the conflict is part of an attempt to purge unwanted minorities from an emerging nation-state. The persecution of minority ethnic groups, such as Jews in Nazi Germany, the Chinese in Vietnam, and the Kurds in Iraq, can be seen as part of a wider systemic process involving the transformation of multiethnic empires into homogeneous nation-states.[19]

Whatever the causes of a particular refugee movement, the consequences of a mass influx can be severe for host countries. To begin with, the demographic impact can be substantial. Greece's population rose about 20 percent when an estimated 1.5 million refugees arrived within a month's time following the Greco-Turkish War of 1922.[20] Today, a significant number of countries have refugee populations that comprise five to ten percent of the total population. For example, one in every eleven people is a refugee in Malawi, the fourth poorest country in the world.[21] Even if the number of refugees is relatively small compared to the total population, the sudden arrival of refugees can create the perception that a country is being "flooded" by foreigners. In 1990, for instance, the Austrian population reacted strongly to rumors that 100,000 Romanians were about to enter the country. Even though only about 2,000 Romanians actually entered the country, this was enough to trigger an outbreak of xenophobia.[22] Public opinion can also become antirefugee if negative perceptions develop about particular refugees groups. American public opinion, for instance, became unfavorable toward granting asylum to Cubans when it became widely known that some of the 130,000 refugees transported to the United States in the Mariela boatlift of 1980 were criminals and mental patients.[23]

For host countries, coping with the humanitarian requirements of a mass exodus can be expensive. The financial costs of refugee relief, maintenance, and resettlement are particularly staggering if one considers that the twenty states with the highest ratio of refugees to the local population have an annual per capita income of less than $700.[24] Even in rich,

industrialized countries, the administrative costs of processing asylum
applictions and of social services can be burdensome. In response to
increasing numbers of arrivals, Belgium, for instance, increased its spend-
ing on asylum-seekers from 300 million francs (US$9.6 million) in 1986
to over two billion (US$ 60 million) in 1990.[25]

Without exception, a major refugee flow from one country to another
also has important political repercussions. Within host countries, the
arrival of large groups of refugees may disrupt an established pattern, such
as a fragile ethnic balance or a stable economy. For instance, the arrival of
Salvadoran refugees into Belize in the 1980s threatened to undermine the
delicate relationship between English and Spanish speakers there. In
Western Europe and North America, the increase in the number of
asylum-seekers from the Third World has been accompanied by increased
xenophobia, racial attacks, and the increased popularity of far-right political parties. A refuge influx can also have international political consequences. Officially, accepting a refugee is a purely humanitarian response.
In fact, assisting refugees is often interpreted by refugee-producing countries as a hostile act. If the influx involves a "refugee warrior community,"
it may involve the host country in violent disputes with the country of
origin. South Africa, for instance, has admitted to attacking refugee
camps in Angola and Zambia.[26] Refugees can also become pawns in global
power struggles, such as that which existed between the East and West
during the Cold War, or used to discredit or destablize an opponent. The
strong support of the United States for refugees from Eastern European
and other Communist countries is a case in point. In some cases, refugees
can become important political actors in their own right; the Palestinians
are the most prominent example of this.

The Root of the Asylum Problem: Immigration Restrictions

In part because of the dramatic consequences of refugee movements on
host countries, virtually all refugees of the twentieth century have faced
enormous problems after leaving their home countries. John Stoessinger
sums up the problem this way: "What distinguishes the refugee of the
twentieth century is the immense difficulty, and often impossibility of
finding a new home."[27] Since World War I international migrants have
found themselves subject to increasing amounts of government regulations: the requirement that all international travelers carry a passport is
the most visible manifestation of this. The relatively free immigration for
Europeans of the nineteenth century abruptly came to an end when many
countries adopted restrictive laws in an attempt to limit the entry of

unwanted ethnic groups, political dissidents, and poor workers. In this regard, the United States led the way with the immigration acts of 1921 and 1924, and was soon followd by Canada, Australia, New Zealand and the republics of Latin America. In the post-1945 era, immigration restrictions have been maintained in all Western countries and increasingly adopted worldwide. Although some countries in the developing world lack the means to police their borders effectively, strict control over frontiers is becoming a worldwide reality.[28]

The development of restrictive immigration policies more than anything else has conditioned the asylum problem in the West. In the nineteenth century the poor and the persecuted of Europe could simply travel to a new country. Since World War I this type of migration has not been allowed. This was most clearly demonstrated in the depression years of the 1930s, when Jewish refugees in flight from Nazi Germany found immigration barriers virtually everywhere they went. The Vietnamese refugees languishing in closed camps in Hong Kong are victims of the same phenomenon: they cannot easily return home, but there is no country willing to accept them permanently. A climate of immigration restrictions also conditions the "asylum crisis" of the 1990s in Western Europe. Although the number of asylum-seekers in Europe was widedly perceived as being extremely large, in fact 450,000 applications is relatively small if one considers that Western Europe's population as a whole is almost 300 million. Nevertheless, any unexpected arrivals have the potential to disrupt normal immigration channels if they are highly regulated. In addition, it is no accident that the "asylum crisis" developed after many Western European governments strictly limited legal means of immigration to their countries in the mid-1970s.

From the above description of refugee and asylum problems, it appears that refugees of the twentieth century have faced incredible difficulties in reestablishing themselves within the normal confines of the international state system. In many cases the causes of refugee movements have precluded refugees from quickly returning to their home countries. Moreover, immigration restrictions have prevented them from simply settling in another neighboring country. But the picture for this century's refugees is not entirely bleak, because refugee movements have attracted the attention of political leaders and have become international issues.[29] As early as 1938, one writer noted that "new means of rapid communication have meant for the refugees that to a certain extent the world is his asylum and the world is concerned with his fate."[30] This statement refers to the development of an international regime, a concept that will be discussed below.

Two International Refugee Regimes

Since World War I responses to refugee movements and asylum problems have been made not only by national governments but also by international institutions. These responses compose an international regime, that is, a series of governing arrangements set up by states at the international level to deal with a specific issue.[31] Since refugees first emerged as a major international issue in the 1920s, there have been two international refugee regimes. The first began in 1921 when the League of Nations first accepted responsibility for assisting Russian refugees and continued until the outbreak of war in 1939. After World War II governments once again realized that new measures would be necessary to assist the refugees and displaced people created by the conflict. The result was the creation of a new international refugee regime, a regime that in its essentials is still in existence today.

Membership and Scope

States always have been the dominant actors in the international refugee regime because they act both as grantors of asylum and as donors for international efforts. The interwar refugee regime's membership approximated that of the League of Nations; it was primarily composed of European and Latin American countries. Though not a member of the League of Nations, the United States occasionally departed from its isolationist foreign policy to support international refugee assitance efforts. The Soviet Union, in contrast, strongly objected to any international efforts aimed at helping refugees. The scope of this regime initially included only Russian refugees but gradually grew to include Greek, Turkish, Bulgarian, Armenian, Assyrian, Assyro-Chaldean, Saar, and German refugees. The regime's scope, however, remained limited to refugees in Europe and European refugees outside of Europe.

The membership and scope of the contemporary refugee regime reflect both the impact of the Cold War and decolonization. Begun in an era of confrontation between the United States and Soviet Union, the United States and its Western allies essentially created the regime. The Soviet Union and its allies in Eastern Europe boycotted international refugee assistance efforts because of fundamental disputes over the repatriation of displaced people after World War II. Like that of its interwar counterpart, the original scope of this regime was restricted to European refugees. The 1951 Refugee Convention, for instance, applies only to those who became refugees before 1 January 1951 and allows governments to further restrict its applicability to events occurring in Europe. Over time, both the membership and scope of the contemporary refugee regime have accommodated the expansion of the international state system. The regime now has a global membership, which includes most of the African, Asian, and Latin American countries that belong to the United Nations. Moreover, its scope includes refugees all over the world, including the Third World. The 1967 Protocol formalizes these changes; it removes any geographic and time restrictions on international refugee assistance.[32]

The Principles and Norms

Despite the differences in scope and membership between the interwar refugee regime and its contemporary counterpart, their underlying principles and norms have remained essentially the same. Both regimes embody a belief in state sovereignty, the supreme authority that states exercise over their territory and population and against outside forces.[33] Applied to refugee issues, the sovereignty principle translates into the authority of a state to control the entry and exit of refugees and their treatment while within the boundaries of the state. Both regimes also contain a humanitarian principle that rests on the belief in the fundamental worth and dignity of all human beings, and that refugee needs should be met in an apolitical, nondiscriminatory fashion.[34] According to one United Nations High Commissioner for Refugees, "In refugee affairs this means that the interest of the refugee or asylum seeker as a human being should take precedence over the possible conflicting interests of states."[35]

Both the interwar and contemporary refugee regimes set norms or standards for the provision of refugee assistance that differentiate refugees from other types of migrants. In this sense, both regimes can be seen as attempts by states to make exceptions in otherwise restrictive immigration policies for those deemed to be especially needy: people who left their home countries not for convenience or economic gain but because their lives were threatened. In carrying out assistance, both regimes assert the norm that all countries have an obligation to assist refugees, not just those directly affected by an influx. In other words, there should be financial burden-sharing.[36] Refugee assistance programs of the 1920 and 1930s especially depended on the financing of two Great Powers, Britain and France, and on widespread popularity among the smaller countries of both Western and Eastern Europe. In the contemporary regime, fulfillment of the burden-sharing norm rests on the willingness of donor countries, especially those in North America and Western Europe, to finance refugee aid operations in Third World countries.

Both the interwar and contemporary refugee regime also include the asylum norm, the right of states to grant sanctuary to any individuals who come to their territory. This norm predates the creation of the first international refugee regime; it has a long history in both state practice and international law.[37] Neither the contemporary nor interwar refugee regimes recognize the right of the individual to be granted asylum. This, in turn, is a reflection of the fact that states created both regimes to solve "refugee problems." These regimes should not be considered radical attempts to guarantee universal human rights but, rather, modest efforts to correct imperfections in the international state system by returning refugees to a secure place within it.

It is interesting to note, however, that at least two concerted attempts have been made to expand the contemporary refugee regime's norms to include an individual right to asylum. In 1948 considerable debate about a right of asylum for individuals took place at the conference preparing the United Nations Declaration of Human Rights. Despite support for such a right, the conference embraced the traditional position on asylum in international law. It adopted Article 14(1), which states that "everyone has the right to seek and to enjoy in other countries asylum from persecution." In using this wording the conference rejected a proposal to include the words "to be granted asylum." In 1968 the right of asylum for the individual was discussed again in an international forum. At the conference on territorial asylum, governments once more failed to agree on a right of asylum for the individual.[38] Despite this failure, the debate over the asylum norm is far from settled because refugee advocates continue to champion an individual right to asylum.

The Institutional Framework

Perhaps the most striking similarity between the interwar and contemporary refugee regimes is that they both center around an intergovernmental organization. From 1921 until 1939, the refugee agencies of the League of Nations served as the focal point for international efforts to assist refugees. In fact, the first High Commissioner, Fridtjof Nansen, set up the institutional framework still used by UNHCR today: a head office in Geneva and a staff of delegates in the major host countries.[39] As High Commissioner, Nansen used his position to make moral and financial appeals on behalf of refugees with governments.[40] Dr. van Heuven Goedhart, the first U.N. High Commissioner for Refugees, also conceptualized his role in this way—as the refugees' representative and the promoter of their interests.[41] Because of the highly personal nature of the office of High Commissioner, the effectiveness of the regime has always depended in part on the character of person who holds it.

The delegates of the High Commissioner for Refugees compose an essential feature of the institutional mechanisms of both the interwar and contemporary refugee regimes. Nansen initially started this system of delegates when he appointed representatives in major refugee host countries. Although the refugee agencies of the League of Nations underwent several structural transformations, this system of delegates remained virtually constant until the outbreak of World War II.[42] When preparing to set up the UNHCR, Dr. van Heuven Goedhart also established a system of delegates, beginning with representatives in eleven countries, primarily in Europe.[43] Today, the UNHCR has more than eighty offices located throughout the world. This system of delegates makes the international refugee regime unique in the field of human rights because it provides an international enforcement mechanism.

Although the office of the High Commissioner has taken on the mantle of refugee advocate, it must not be forgotten that both the League of Nations and the United Nations have as their members sovereign states. Both the refugee agencies of the League and the United Nations have been formally independent, but they have always been dependent on governments for donations. While the League of Nations was prepared to pay the basic administrative expenses of the refugee agencies, it never accepted a permanent commitment to finance emergency relief or permanent settlement: this was considered the job of governments and private, voluntary organizations. As a result of this philosophy, Nansen began on a shoestring budget of 1,500 pounds and the tasking of caring for more than one million Russian refugees. Nansen sought to compensate for meager resources by using his considerable skills as a fundraiser.[44] Although some governments, primarily the United States, allocated funds directly to the International Refugee Organization (IRO) so that it could resettle refugees and displaced persons after World War II, they also discontinued this financing mechanism when they created its successor. The statutes of the UNHCR make it clear that the United Nations will only pay its administrative expenses directly. As a result, the UNHCR must continually solicit voluntary contributions from governments for material aid.[45]

Thirty years after Nansen, Dr. van Heuven Goedhart began his work in three empty rooms in the Palais des Nations in Geneva with a budget of $300,000, not even enough to pay the administrative expenses of the fledgling organization. Quickly realizing the need for additional funding for material assistance to refugees, the High Commissioner urged the

General Assembly to establish a special emergency fund, which it reluctantly did in February 1952, over the objections of the United States delegation.[46] Other High Commissioners have followed his lead. When the UNHCR faced a serious shortfall of funds due to the pressures of assisting increasing numbers of refugees in Africa, Asia, and Latin America in the mid-1980s, High Commissioner Poul Hartling appealed to governments, saying, "We are not crying wolf, it is a bad situation. . . . We cannot print our own money, we cannot steal it and we are not allowed to borrow it. We have to get it from governments."[47] In March 1990, High Commissioner Thorvald Stoltenberg pointed out that although the number of refugees in the world had doubled in the previous decade, funding had not. He said that "levels of care are falling. I have only half the resources per refugee today that we had in 1980."[48]

The continual financial problems of international organizations dealing with refugees are due in part to the constraints placed on them by their founders. In agreeing to aid Russian refugees, League members withheld permanent funding because they conceptualized refugee assistance as a temporary project.[49] In debates over the statutes of the UNHCR, the U.S. delegate, Mrs. Eleanor Roosevelt, argued that the organization should essentially be an international deliberative body, not an international relief agency. In a related argument, the U.S. delegation contended that the refugee problem was essentially a temporary one. Consequently, the international agency set up to deal with refugees should have a temporary mandate.[50] Given the persistence of refugee emergencies since World War I, the assumption that refugees are a temporary problem has been shown to be incorrect. Nevertheless, the structure of the UNHCR, the key institution in the contemporary international refugee regime, still reflects the desire of governments to maintain strict controls over the organization and to limit their financial commitment to refugees.

The Crucial Role of INGOS and NGOs

International nongovernmental organizations (INGOs) have been crucial actors in the international refugee regime since its creation. In fact, Gustave Ador of the International Committee of the Red Cross first drew the attention of the League of Nations to refugee issues when he called on the Council as "the only supranational political authority capable of solving a problem which is beyond the power of exclusively humanitarian organisations" to assist Russian refugees.[51] Once appointed as High Commissioner, Nansen set up an advisory committee of private organizations composed of two major types of INGOs: (1) general-purpose organizations that helped refugees as one of their functions, such as the Save the Children Fund and the Society of Friends, and (2) organizations designed to assist members of a particular nationality, such as the Russian Red Cross and the Armenian Benevolent Union. These INGOs distinguished themselves as the primary providers of emergency relief and social services to refugees in the years when the modern European welfare state was in embryo.[52] In the 1930s the role of Jewish INGOs was particularly important because of the unwillingness of governments to forgo appeasement and directly aid refugees fleeing Nazi Germany.[53]

The statutes of the UNHCR specifically encourage the High Commissioner to establish links and coordinate the activities of private organizations assisting refugees.[54] Today, the UNHCR's NGO Liaison Unit maintains close contact with more than 250 NGOs worldwide. According to Robert Gorman, private, voluntary organizations are involved in "virtually every state of the refugee relief and development process," including emergency relief, long-term care and maintenance, and resettlement. Despite their importance, these agencies are not at the "heart of the decision-making process, but rather serve as the volunteers who implement the relief decisions made by others."[55] In this respect, the role of INGOs has changed over time. In the interwar years, INGOs had greater capacity to shape refugee assistance projects, partly because their financial resources were greatly needed.

The Rules of the Regime

Both the interwar and contemporary international refugee regimes contain rules designed to enforce their major principles and norms. The exact content of these rules, however, has varied considerably over time. The most notable difference between the interwar and postwar refugee regimes concerns the definition of a refugee. This is an important issue because definitions written into international law have a special function: they establish obligations of states toward refugees and entitle those granted refugee status to certain benefits.[56] The definition of a refugee in fact determines who is and who it not eligible for assistance at any given time, a decision that in some circumstances can make the difference between life and death.

The League of Nations defined refugees according to group affiliation. The 1933 Refugee Convention, for instance, defined a Russian refugee as anyone who was of Russian origin and did not enjoy the diplomatic protection of the USSR and had not acquired another nationality.[57] The interwar practice of defining refugees on a group basis had several advantages. From a purely practical point of view, it provided a relatively efficient way of extending refugee status to a large number of refugees. In addition, the granting of refugee status did not depend on individual refugees proving they left their home countries because of political persecution. Instead, the group designation gave refugee status to people who fled a variety of life-threatening situations. The Russian refugees, for instance, included all of the following types of people: victims of the Russian and Ukrainian famines of 1921–23; peasants fleeing both the Red and White armies in the Russian civil war; soldiers of the White armies and their families; and former czarist officials and aristocrats.

Despite the merits of group designation, this method of defining refugees had one major disadvantage: the system lent itself to open political debates about which refugee groups should be assisted. At the 1933 Assembly, for instance, the German delegation strongly opposed any material assistance being given to Jews and political dissidents fleeing the Third Reich. This objection, combined with the desire of Britain and French governments to appease Germany, resulted in a relatively weak response by the League of Nations to this refugee exodus.[58] Obviously, public debates between government officials about the merits of specific refugee groups have great potential for politicization, a fact increasingly recognized by both scholars and government officials in the mid-1930s.[59] After World War II momentum for the creation of a universal definition of a refugee grew. With this trend came an increasing emphasis of the causes of a refugee's flight, a reflection of the dramatic impact of the Nazi era on thinking about human rights; in many minds, refugees became synonymous with victims of Nazi persecution. As a result, refugees tended to be thought of as individuals facing persecution for their religious or political beliefs, or because of their association with a particular class or racial group. Jacques Vernant's study of postwar refugees clearly illustrates this change in thinking. According to Vernant, "Before a man can be described as a refugee, the political events which cause him to leave, or to break with, the State to which he owed allegiance must be defined. Thus political events which in the country of origin led to his departure must be accompanied by persecution or by the threat of persecution against himself or at least against a section of the population with which he identifies himself."[60]

In keeping with current thinking about refugees, the founders of the UNHCR tried to produce a general definition applicable to all refugees.[61] The end results of their negotiations, the 1951 Refugee Convention, defines a refugee as any person who has left his home country "owing to well-founded fear of being persecuted for reasons of race, religion, nationality, membership of a particular social group or political opinion . . ."[62] By adopting this definition the creators of the 1951 Convention hoped to end debate on the question "Who is a refugee?" Nevertheless, controversy quickly arose because the convention does not define what constitutes persecution. This omission leaves open the following question: Should economic deprivation be treated as a form of persecution? This question has been increasingly asked now that many refugees come from the materially poorer Southern countries to relatively richer Northern ones. Some refugee advocates contend that "economic refugees," those fleeing poverty and governments unable to provide for their people, should be considered victims of persecution.[63] In practice, governments have been very reluctant to equate economic deprivation with persecution.

The 1951 Convention's focus on individuals who have fled their home countries has also been challenged. To begin with, the utility and justness of the 1951 Convention's exclusion of people displaced within their own country from refugee status has been questioned, given that international refugees may be only one part of a migration generated by war, civil war, or economic breakdown.[64] In addition, many refugees from civil wars involving guerrilla warfare fail the "persecution" litmus test. They may simply be people who flee to escape an invading army or "crossfire refugees" who run from both sides in a civil war to escape violence. The incidence of man-made disasters, especially famine that can accompany warfare, has also prompted a reevaluation of what constitutes a natural disaster.[65] The Organization of African Unity has developed a definition of a refugee that includes people in flight "owing to external aggression, occupation, foreign domination or events seriously disturbing public order," but it is not applicable to non-OAU member states.[66] The United Nations General Assembly (UNGA) has, however, accomplished a similar task by authorizing UNHCR to deal with specified groups in UNGA resolutions. Ironically, this return to group definitions is reminiscent of methods used by the League of Nations to cope with large refugee movements.

However the term "refugee" is defined in international law, the fact remains that this definition must be implemented by governments and international agencies. Often this process falls prey to political and strategic considerations rather than purely humanitarian ones. Vernant identified this problem in the early postwar era and urged that "a kind of international arbiter as free as possible of the shackles of national pressure and ideological bias" be allowed to determine refugee status.[67] Despite the existence of an international organization with this responsibility, problems continue. A former UNHCR official, Gilbert Jaeger, contends that government officials are very creative in circumventing U.N. definitions when they desire to stem a mass refugee flow.[68] In addition, Gil Loescher and John Scanlan have documented that U.S. refugee admissions policy has shown a clear preference for refugees from Communist enemies rather than from authoritarian allies.[69] The continuing difficulties in ensuring adherence to international law indicates that the "perfect" refugee definition may not automatically bring about humanitarian resolutions to refugee problems.

The 1933 and 1951 Conventions also lay out other rules concerning the treatment of refugees in host countries for the interwar and contemporary refugee regimes, respectively. Of these rules, by far the most important is the rule of non-refoulement, the "prohibition of the forcible return of a refugee to a country of persecution."[70] Article 3 of the 1933 Convention sets forth the provision that states should refrain from expelling or refusing entry to refugees authorized to live in their territory unless "national security or public order" required it. The 1951 Convention represents an improvement over this earlier rule. Article 33 incorporates non-refoulement as a cornerstone of the legal protection of refugees. While this rule does not establish a refugee's right to be granted asylum—this remains the prerogative of governments—it does provide a limited form of asylum because it prohibits the return or refugees to their country of origin.

Responses to International Refugee Movements

Since 1921 the actors in the international refugee regimes have dealt with a variety of refugee movements. A key element in any international response is the granting of temporary asylum to refugees, a decision that has been left almost entirely to the governments of individual states. As stated above, neither regime recognizes the right of an individual to be granted asylum. In the twentieth century, the most acute refugee problems have occurred when no state was willing to grant asylum to a particular group; the classic example of this is the plight of Jewish refugees in the late 1930s. International institutions have had only mixed success in encouraging governments to accept refugees. In 1938 President Franklin Roosevelt invited forty governments to a special meeting to deal the mass exodus from the Third Reich. The Evian conference produced few tangible results because governments refused to make definite commitments to accept refugees. As a consequence of this, Evian has become a symbol of the failure of international efforts to help Jewish refugees.[71] It is important to remember, however, that countries did offer asylum to the vast majority of refugees of the 1920s and 1930s. Even in the case of Jewish refugees, more than 400,000 people, approximately one-half of the 1933 Jewish population of Germany, successfully found asylum in another country.[72]

During the Cold War, the asylum record of Western governments has improved. The 1979 U.N. conference on Vietnamese refugees stands in stark contrast to the failed Evian conference. It resulted in firm commitments by governments to accept more than a quarter million refugees for permanent resettlement.[73] In addition, Western governments consistently provided asylum for refugees from Eastern Europe and the Soviet Union throughout the Cold War. One of the major reasons for this change is that most Western country's now have special provisions for refugees in their immigration policies.[74] Before World War II, in contrast, refugees were not considered separate from ordinary migrants in immigration. The development of refugee quotas, while not a complete solution to asylum problems, is a very important step and can be seen as a product of the gradual development of international refugee law giving refugees a special status in international and municipal law.

Since the 1980s the Western tradition of asylum has become increasingly under siege. In response to dramatic increases in the number of arrivals, European governments have adopted policies of "humane deterrence" toward asylum-seekers. These measures include more restrictive interpretations of the definition of a refugee, rejections of refugees at the border on the grounds that they should have sought asylum in a different country, sanctions on airlines transporting undocumented persons, and reductions in social benefits available to asylum-seekers. Germany and the Netherlands, for instance, have placed asylum-seekers in restricted housing. These policies, while within the prerogatives of states, violate the humanitarian spirit of the international refugee regime.[75] Governments in the rich North have also increasingly labeled asylum-seekers from the poor South as economic migrants. The United States government, for isntance, only grudgingly consented to providing refugees from the civil war in El Salvador with a Temporary Protected Status in 1990, almost ten years after large numbers of Salvadorans began arriving.[76] Today, the French government rejects about 80 to 85 percent of the asylum claims it receives on the grounds that the seekers are not bona fide refugees.[77] Unfortunately, most intergovernmental cooperation on this issue has focused on ways of stemming the flow of refugees, rather than on ensuring asylum to those who need it.[78]

Legal Protection

Although states are extremely important in granting asylum and providing refugees assistance, the concrete manifestations of the international refugee regime's assistance and burden-sharing norms are the programs of IGOs. It is through international agencies like the High Commission for Refugees that donor governments channel funds to governments directly coping with a refugee influx. The earliest and most persistent concern of international institutions established to assist refugees is the legal protection of refugees. When Gustave Ador initially appealed to the League of Nations in 1921, he identified the need for a High Commissioner to define the "legal position of the Russian refugees."[79] The statutes of the the UNHCR stress that a major function of the organization should be "providing international protection" to refugees.[80] Legal protection has been a crucial function of both the interwar and contemporary refugee regimes because of the peculiar legal status of refugees. Outside their home countries, often without documentation, refugees may be unable legally to travel, work, marry, or attend schools. More important, they may be subject to violence by officials of their host government, and even expulsion back to a country where their lives would be in danger. In order to counter these legal disabilities, the office of the High Commissioner for Refugees is extremely important.

In 1922, High Commissioner Nansen pioneered the development of the "Nansen passport system," a system of internationally recognized travel documents that enabled refugees to cross international borders legally. Moreover, the High Commissioner's delegates provided consular services for refugees, and even intervened with governments to prevent the expulsion of refugees. In 1935, for instance, the Nansen International Office reported that it had made more than 3,000 interventions on behalf of refugees.[81] Today, the UNHCR essentially continues these two functions. Each of its offices worldwide has a team of protection officers, charged with promoting the application of the 1951 Convention by governments and intervening on the behalf of refugees when necessary. The UNHCR's role in legal protection, however, has not been without controversy. Human rights organizations recently called attention to the UNHCR's role in regard to Vietnamese refugees in Hong Kong, charging that it represented the government and failed to protect refugees.[82] This incident indicates the important, though unofficial, role INGOs also play in securing refugee protection.[83]

Emergency Relief, Refugee Maintenance, and Durable Solutions

It seems obvious that an initial concern in any refugee emergency must be meeting the basic needs of refugees for food, shelter, clothing and medical care. Nevertheless, governments have consistently been reluctant to endow an international organization with these responsibilities. In 1921, High Commissioner Nansen faced this dilemma while dealing with the plight of 40,000 Russian refugees dumped in Constantinople. Nansen disregarded his mandate from the League of Nations and organized relief efforts because "it seemed to me useless to endeavour to find productive employment for people who were actually starving."[84] In the 1950s, the first UN High Commissioner once again fought for the funds to provide emergency services. Dr. van Heuvan Goedhart pointed out "What does international protection mean for a man who dies of hunger? Passports are necessary but hunger can't be stilled with them." Because of his urgings, the UNGA established an emergency fund to materially assist refugees.[85]

Once the basic material and legal needs of refugees are met, other measures aimed at assisting them can be undertaken. In the 1920s, Nansen spoke of providing "final solutions" for refugees. The statutes of the UNHCR refer to seeking "permanent solutions." More recently, the term "durable solutions" has come to refer to measures that enable refugees either to return home or become self-sufficient and fully integrated into a new country. The major actors in the international refugee regime have always considered voluntary repatriation to be the most desirable durable solution to any refugee movement. After all, repatriation allows the refugees to return to their home countries. It also removes financial and social burdens from host and donor governments, as they need not provide for refugees on a permanent basis. In appointing Nansen as High Commissioner, the League of Nations specifically charged him with the task of arranging the repatriation of Russian refugees. The statutes of the UNHCR also specifically call on the High Commissioner to facilitate the voluntary repatriation of refugees.[86]

Despite widespread agreement that repatriation is the best durable solution to a refugee problem, it has not provided a panacea. While it is true that refugees from wars of national liberation usually returned home quickly after the achievement of independence, in many cases the nature of a particular conflict makes repatriation extremely difficult. If persecution based on race, religion, or ethnicity forces a minority group to flee, repatriation may be virtually impossible. If a revolution or civil war forced refugees to leave, long-term political changes are necessary before they can safely return home.

The governmental preference for repatriation has meant that international organizations have actively promoted this solution since the 1920s. High Commissioner Nansen, for instance, spent three years negotiating a repatriation agreement with the Soviet Union that resulted in only 6,000 refugees returning home.[87] This program was abruptly terminated when the Soviet mission responsible for arranging repatriation from Bulgaria was charged with espionage. In addition, segments of the Russian exile community strongly objected to the repatriation efforts and sharply criticized Nansen for arranging it. Though Nansen rode out this storm, the controversy discouraged further efforts in this era.[88]

The UNHCR arranges repatriation by concluding triparite agreements between it, the host country, and the home country. Although these programs have had some succeses, critics argue that putting the UNHCR in the middle is "ponderous, time-consuming, and produces poor results." In some circumstances, one hundred refugees may spontaneously repatriate for every one who returns with the help of UNHCR. Moreover, tripartite arrangements allow no direct participation for refugees.[89] Though officially the UNHCR promotes only voluntary repatriation, it has been criticized for promoting repatriation to unsafe countries, such as the 1986–87 return of refugees from Djibouti to Ethiopia. The persistence of controversies over repatriation stems from this paradox: international organizations are charged with assisting refugees, yet they are the creatures of governments and must respond to their desires.

If repatriation proves impossible in the short run, other solutions must be found for refugees. Increasingly, refugee advocates and government officials have argued that assistance should go beyond the maintenance of refugee populations. Instead, aid should promote economic development in the host country and include both refugees and the local population. In 1983 then High Commissioner Poul Hartling initiated a study on refugees and development. In October 1984 the executive committee of the UNHCR endorsed the results of this study, a program of action that called for linkages between refugee aid and development. Another important intergovernmental meeting, the Second International Conference on Assistance to Refugees in Africa (ICARA II) held in July 1984, focused on projects that would improve infrastructure for refugees and their African host countries. Based on these ideas, the UNHCR has sponsored a number of development-oriented assistance projects. For instance, it collaborated with the World Bank on development projects aimed at increasing employment opportunities for Afghan refugees and providing needed roads and irrigation systems for Pakistan.[90] In 1991 High Commissioner Sadako Ogata affirmed the U.N.'s role in development. According to her, the UNHCR "is not a development agency, but we should act as an advocate of development assistance."[91]

Although linking refugee aid with development was introduced as a new concept in the 1980s, in fact this approach dates to the 1920s. The refugee agencies of the League of Nations did not use the term "development," but they pioneered international efforts in this area. In 1924 the League of Nations established the Greek Refugee Settlement Commission, an agency composed of Greek government officials, Greek refugees, and League of Nations advisers, which helped settle about 600,000 Greek refugees in what is today Greek Macedonia. The project included establishing villages, teaching agricultural techniques, and building infrastructure. The League sponsored similar programs for ethnic Bulgar refugees in Bulgaria and for Armenian refugees in Greece and the Middle East.[92] All these projects combined development with refugee assistance and aimed at integrating refugees with the local population of a particular area.

Despite its desirability, facilitating local integration can be extremely difficult. For one, host governments have to be willing to accept refugees on a long-term or permanent basis. In addition, development projects can be expensive. The League of Nations financed its projects by facilitating international loans for host governments and through voluntary contributions. Even so, elaborate plans for a refugee settlement scheme in Soviet Armenia collapsed because of lack of funding. Similarly, the Africa governments at ICARA II presented plans for more than 150 projects, but funding offers fell far short of this goal.[93] Meanwhile, the UNHCR faces chronic funding shortages; from 1980 to 1990, the number of refugees nearly doubled, from 8.2 million to 15 million, yet the UNHCR's budget remained constant.[94]

The UNHCR also promotes resettlement in a third country as a durable solution. A classic example is the resettlement of Indochinese throughout the world in the late 1970s. The United States alone accepted almost a million people for resettlement. In the past, resettlement gave opportunities to European refugees displaced by World War II. It also helped to provide employment for refugees in the 1920s; the League of Nations ran an international employment service that settled about 50,000 Armenian and Russian refugees from Eastern European countries in France and Belgium.[95] Despite many examples of successful resettlement, this particular durable solution has limited applicability because of its high costs. The United States, for instance, spends only twelve dollars per refugee overseas, while it spends about $4,700 on each refugee admission.[96] In addition, overseas resettlement takes people far away from their native lands, climates, and cultures, which in turn may complicate assimilation.

The Issue of Root Causes

Given the many problems created by prolonged relief, repatriation, local integration, and resettlement, it is worthwhile to consider why more effort has not been made to prevent the creation of refugees in the first place. In this regard, the first High Commissioner for Refugees set a precedent that continues to this day. Nansen interpreted the humanitarian principle to mean that his office must remain politically neutral if it was to be effective in providing refugees assistance. Though Nansen himself blamed the Turkish government for the creation of Greek and Armenian refugees, he took pains not to let this affect his work. While in the Near East conducting relief operations, Nansen wrote that "I cannot in any way denounce the proceeding of the Turkish authorities, whatever my personal opinion may be. I am obliged to confine myself to appealing on strictly humanitarian grounds for assistance for the refugees."[97]

In contrast to Nansen, James G. McDonald, High Commissioner for Refugees coming from Germany, believed that assisting refugees necessitated addressing the causes of a refugee movement, even if it meant censoring a government. After futile attempts to assist Jewish refugees from the Third Reich, McDonald officially resigned in December 1935. In his letter of resignation he called on the League of Nations to "remove or mitigate the causes which create German refugees, "and argued that "considerations of diplomatic correctness must yield to this of common humanity."[98] Although the Western press widely acclaimed McDonald's letter, his proposal received a cold reception at the League of Nations. The League's council rejected any intrusion into what it considered to be Germany's internal affairs and appointed a more docile replacement.[99] In a press interview, Sir Neill Malcolm, a former British military officer, declared that "I have no policy, but the policy of the League is to deal with the political and legal status of the refugees. It has nothing to do with the domestic policy of Germany."[100]

The founders of the UNHCR clearly followed the Nansen model when they established the organization. The UNHCR's statutes define the work of the High Commissioner to be "of an entirely non-political character."[101] Presumably, the political organs of the United Nations are charged with the political settlement of disputes. This provision reflects the desire of states in the international refugee regime to uphold the principle of state sovereignty, defined as freedom from external interference. Nevertheless, the issue of root causes continues to surface. In 1981, for instance, the High Commissioner for Refugees, Sadruddin Aga Khan, conducted a study on the causes of mass exoduses that emphasized underdevelopment as a fundamental cause of refugee movements in the South.[102] In 1985 U.S. High Commissioner Jean-Pierre Hocke called for more attention to be paid to the issue of root causes in refugee movements. He argued that such concern was essential if repatriation efforts were to succeed and were not necessarily incompatible with the UNHCR's humanitarian role.[103] Shortly after her appointment in 1991, High Commissioner Ogata affirmed that "an effective and humanitarian approach to the refugee issue must focus on causes as much as effects."[104] The continued debate among the actors of the international refugee regime about the issue of root causes indicates that refugee assistance efforts cannot be completely separated from the broader concerns of human rights and conflict resolution.

Conclusion

In the seventy-year history of organized international assistance to refugees, major political changes have had a dramatic impact on refugee issues. The formation of the League of Nations in the aftermath of World War I provided the catalyst for international effort to provide passports to Russian refugees, arrange jobs for Armenian refugees, and sponsor settlements for Greek refugees. Similarly, the Cold War atmosphere has profoundly shaped the membership, scope, and functions of the current international refugee regime. If the past serves as a guide to the future, we should expect the decline of the Cold War and other global changes to bring both new challenges and new opportunities for international refugee assistance. What is uncertain is *how* current international institutions concerned with refugees will adapt to this new environment. The great danger for refugees is that these institutions will become increasingly ineffective and eventually collapse, as was the case in the late 1930s. If international institutions are to respond successfully to the challenges of the 1990s, a number of issues needs to be addressed. In this process, the role of Western countries is particularly important because they originally founded the regime and continue to be among its key supporters.

To begin with, the assumption that refugees are a temporary problem should be seriously reevaluated. The continued persistence of refugee movements and asylum problems since World War I strongly suggests that the founders of the interwar and contemporary refugee regimes operated on a fundamentally wrong assumption. Far from being a temporary problem that can be easily solved, refugees are a continuing issue requiring complex responses. Given the high probability of increasing numbers of refugees in the future, this change is even more imperative. Moreover, the temporary approach to refugee aid is one of the key factors that mitigates against placing the UNHCR and other international refugee agencies on a solid financial footing.

The membership of the current international refugee regime also needs to be reconsidered to take into account the newly emerging democracies of Eastern Europe. Czechoslovakia, Hungary, Poland, and other countries of Eastern Europe played an active role in refugee programs sponsored by the League of Nations, and they could do so again. Already Hungary has become the first former Eastern bloc country to ratify the 1951 Refugees Convention. The UNHCR has also sponsored training seminars for immigration officials in Eastern Europe. These measures need to be strengthened and expanded if the Cold War division between East and West is to be truly closed.

Another crucial issue concerns the Western tradition of asylum. Any effort to preserve this tradition in the face of pressures to cut off the flow of asylum-seekers must recognize the important link between refugee status and international migration. Treating refugees as a special type of migrant only makes sense within the context of a broader immigration policy. Since 1985 the number of asylum-seekers in Europe has been greater than the number of legally admitted foreign workers.[105] In practice, Europe already is a continent of immigration, even if its leaders and people do not think of it in this way.[106] For the Western tradition of asylum to be maintained, a refugee policy must be forged in conjunction with provisions for economic migration. These measures are especially important because of the changes in border controls in EC countries that 1992 will bring.

In the future, the UNHCR and other refugee agencies will increasingly be confronted with calls to expand their services to new types of refugees, including environmental refugees, economic refugees, and displaced people. Given this, it might reasonably be asked if there is still a need for a special refugee agency. In the 1920s government seriously considered a proposal for an International Relief Union that would assist all victims of disasters, including famine, floods, epidemics, and forced migrations. This effort, however, failed, primarily because it saddled governments with "an absolute rather than incremental declaration of international obligations."[107] The IRU proposal also failed to meet the special needs of refugees, which are different from those of other disaster victims. Increased cooperation between the UNHCR and other U.N. agencies might be a way to combine protecting the special needs of refugees and cope with the complexities of a mass exodus. Perhaps one model for the future is the UNHCR's role in assisting Kurdish refugees in 1991. In this disaster, the UNHCR managed refugees camps, the World Food Program provided food, and UNICEF and the World Health Organization supplied medicine, all under the direction of a special Disaster Relief Coordinator.

The issue of root causes is another that confronts the actors in the international refugee regime. It is unlikely that the UNHCR will be able to maintain a purely humanitarian role given the nature of refugee movements and solutions to them. Arranging repatriation, for instance, clearly involves a political determination that a country is safe for return. Using an early-warning mechanism, that is, monitoring human rights conditions with an eye toward preventing and predicting refugee flows, also involves the UNHCR in political issues. Recently the UNHCR has encouraged potential refugees in Albania to stay in the country and fight for increased democratization. A new approach may also be signaled by the Kurdish exodus. In this case, allied forces provided a protective zone within Iraq for Kurdish refugees. It remains to be seen, however, how far these efforts can go without a triggering response by states to protect their sovereignty.

It has never been easy for international institutions dealing with refugees to adjust to major political, economic, and social changes. Virtually all solutions to refugee problems are problematic in some way. IGOs and INGOs are highly constrained in their activities by the desire of states to control both their borders and their financial expenditures. Nevertheless, the history of the interwar and contemporary refugee regimes provides examples of the flexibility that is needed today. The first High Commissioner for Refugees continually disregarded his official mandate in order to meet the emergency and long-term needs of refugees. In the 1950s and 1960s the UNHCR expanded its narrow European focus to help refugees in the developing world. The challenge of the 1990s will be to reshape current ideas and institutions without abandoning traditional commitments to humanitarian principles.

Notes

1. Jonas Widgren, "International Migration and Regional Stability," *International Affairs* (October 1990): 762.
2. "The Year of the Refugee," *Economist* (23 December 1989): 23.
3. See, for instance, the comments of Dr. Peter Nobel, Sweden's first Discrimination Ombudsman in "Refugees and Racism," *Refugees* (December 1987): 35.
4. W. R. Smyser, "Refugees: A Never-Ending Story," *Foreign Affairs* (Fall 1985): 155.
5. Sir John Hope Simpson, *The Refugee Problem: Report of a Survey* (London, 1939), 551.
6. Michael R. Marrus, *The Unwanted: European Refugees in the Twentieth Century* (Oxford, 1985), 297 and 52.
7. Louise Holborn, *Refugees: A Problem of Our Time: the Work of the United Nations High Commissioner for Refugees, 1951–1972* (Metuchen, N.J., 1975), vol. 1, 825–33.
8. U.S. Committee for Refugees, *World Refugee Survey: 1988 in Review* (Washington, D.C., 1989), 32–36.
9. Widgren, "International Migration," 757.
10. Jonas Widgren, "Asylum Policy at a Turning Point," *Refugees* (March 1990): 23.

11. Jodi Jacobson, *Environmental Refugees: A Yardstick of Habitability*, Worldwatch Paper 86 (November 1988): 6.

12. Simpson, *The Refugee Problem*, 5.

13. Ibid., 5–6. Louise Holborn supports this conclusion in *The International Refugee Organization, a Specialized Agency of the United Nations, Its History and Work: 1946–1952* (London, 1956), 1.

14. Leon Gordenker, *Refugees in International Politics* (New York, 1987), 74–75.

15. Marrus, *The Unwanted*, 7–8 and 51.

16. Aristide R. Zolberg, Astri Suhrke, and Sergio Aguayo, *Escape From Violence: Conflict and the Refugee Crisis in the Developing World* (New York, 1989), 245–57.

17. Kathleen Newland, *Refugees: The New International Politics of Displacement*, Worldwatch Paper 43 (March 1981): 5–6.

18. Zolberg et al. *Escape From Violence*, 260–63.

19. Aristide R. Zolberg, "The Formation of New States as a Refugee-Generating Process," *Annals* 467 (May 1983): 24–38.

20. On the Greek exodus, see Stephan Ladas, *The Exchange of Minorities: Bulgaria, Greece, and Turkey* (New York, 1933).

21. *World Refugee Survey, 1989*, 47.

22. "Austria: Hopes and Fear," *Refugees* (July–August 1990): 7.

23. Gil Loescher and John A. Scanlan, *Calculated Kindness: Refugees and America's Half-Open Door, 1945–Present* (New York, 1986), 170.

24. Independent Commission on International Humanitarian issues, *Refugees: Dynamics of Displacement* (London, 1986), 16.

25. "Belgium: Unresolved problems," *Refugees* (March 1991): 18.

26. Elly-Elikunda Mtango, "Military and Armed Attacks on Refugee Camps," in Gil Loescher and Laila Monahan, eds., *Refugees and International Relations* (Oxford, 1989), 93.

27. John G. Stoessinger, *The Refugee and the World Community* (Minneapolis, 1956), 6.

28. See Alan Dowty, *Closed Borders: The Contemporary Assault on Freedom of Movement* (New Haven, 1987).

29. Holborn, *The International Refugee Organization*, 4–5; Marrus, *The Unwanted*, 14.

30. Simpson, *The Refugee Problem*, 10.

31. See Stephen Krasner, ed., *International Regimes* (Ithaca: 1983).

32. Guy S. Goodwin-Gill, *The Refugee in International Law* (Oxford, 1983), 12–13.

33. Hedley Bull, *The Anarchical Society* (London, 1977), 8.

34. Bruce Nichols, "Rubberhand Humanitarianism," *Ethics and International Affairs* 1 (1987): 194.

35. Jean-Pierre Hocke, "Beyond Humanitarianism: The Need for Political Will to Resolve Today's Refugee Problem," address delivered at Oxford University on 20 October 1986 as the Inaugural Joyce Pearce Memorial Lecture (Oxford: Refugee Studies Programme with the Ockenden Venture, 1986), 8.

36. League of Nations, Committee on International Assistance to Refugees, "Report by the Committee Submitted to the Council of the League of Nations" (Geneva: 3 January 1936) [C.2.M.2.1936.XII], esp. 3–5 and 8. See also Holborn, *UNHCR*, 62–64.

37. Atle Grahl-Madsen, *Territorial Asylum* (London, 1980), 3.

38. Goodwin-Gill, *The Refugee in International Law*, 104–14; Atle Grahl-Madsen, *The Status of Refugees in International Law* (Leyden, 1972), 2:6–11.

39. Louise Holborn, "The League of Nations and the Refugee Problem," *Annals of the American Academy of Political and Social Science* 203 (May 1939): 124–35.

40. For a general biography of Nansen, see Jan Sorenson, *The Saga of Fridtjof Nansen* (London, 1932). On his work as High Commissioner, see Claudena Skran, "Profiles of the First Two High Commissioners," *Journal of Refugees Studies* 1 (1988): 277–96.

41. Holborn, *UNHCR*, 105.

42. From 1921 until his death in 1929, Nansen served as High Commissioner for

Refugees. The Refugee Section of the ILO assisted him in his work from 1924 until 1929. From 1931 and 1938, the Nansen International Office was the League's principal agency dealing with refugees. In addition, the League created a special High Commissioner to deal with refugees from Germany, which operated from 1933 until 1938. In 1939 the League merged these two functions and placed all refugees under a single High Commissioner for Refugees once again. Hans Aufrict, *Guide to League of Nations Publications, 1920–1947* (New York, 1951), 190–92.

43. Holborn, *UNHCR*, 106–7.

44. Holborn, *Annals:* 134; Simpson, *The Refugee Problem*, 195.

45. Statute of the Office of the United Nations High Commissioner for Refugees, adopted by the General Assembly on 14 December 1950. A/RES/428(V), Art. 20.

46. Holborn, *UNHCR*, 104–5, 138–39.

47. *Refugees* (November 1985): 9.

48. Paul Lewis, "U.N. Aide Fears Help for Refugees Will Fall Short," *New York Times*, 18 March 1990, 27.

49. Simpson, *The Refugee Problem*, 192.

50. Holborn, *UNHCR*, 68–70.

51. League of Nations, *Official Journal* (March–April 1921): 227–28.

52. Simpson, *The Refugee Problem*, 172–80.

53. Arieh Tartakower and Kurt R. Grossman, *The Jewish Refugees* (New York, 1944), 429–500.

54. *UNHCR Statute*, Article 8, para. (h) and (i).

55. Robert F. Gorman, "Private Voluntary Organizations in Refugee Relief," in Elizabeth Ferris, *Refugees and World Politics* (New York, 1985), 85 and 102.

56. Goodwin-Gill, *The Refugee in International Law*, 2.

57. "Convention relating to the International Status of Refugees, 28 October 1933," *League of Nations Treaty Series*, no. 3663, vol. 159, 203; "Convention Concerning the Status of Refugees coming from Germany, 10 February 1938," *LNTS*, no. 4461, vol. 192, 59.

58. League of Nations, *Official Journal, Special Supplement No. 117, Fourteenth Assembly, Second Committee* (Geneva, 1933), 22–29; Timothy P. Maga, "Closing the Door: The French Government and Refugee Policy, 1933–1939," *French Historical Studies* 12 (Spring 1982): 432.

59. In 1936, for instance, the Institute for International Law developed a universal definition of a refugee. In 1935 the Norwegian Foreign Minister championed an unsuccessful proposal that the League of Nations create a single refugee organization to deal with all refugees. Atle Grahl-Madsen, *The Status of Refugees in International Law*, 1:74, and League of Nations, *Official Journal, Special Supplement No. 143, Sixteenth Assembly, Sixth Committee* (Geneva, 1935), 10–14, 52–54.

60. Jacques Vernant, *The Refugee in the Post-War World* (London, 1953), 6.

61. Holborn, *UNHCR*, 65–86.

62. "United Nations Convention Relating to the Status of Refugees, 28 July 1951," *UNTS*, no. 2545, vol. 189, 152.

63. See, for instance, Charles Keely, *Global Refugee Policy: The Case for a Development-Oriented Strategy* (New York, 1981), 13 and 19.

64. Lance Clark, "Internal Refugees—The Hidden Half," in *World Refugee Survey—1988 in Review* (Washington D.C., 1989); 18–24.

65. See Amartya Sen, *Poverty and Famines* (Oxford, 1981), and Independent Commission on International Humanitarian Issues, *Famine: A Man-made Disaster?* (London, 1985).

66. "OAU Convention Governing the Specific Aspects of Refugee Problems in Africa of September 10, 1968," *UNTS*, no. 14691, Art. 1(2).

67. Vernant, *The Refugee in the Post-War World*, 7–8.

68. Gilbert Jaeger, "The Definition of 'Refugee': Restrictive vs. Expanding Trends," *World Refugee Survey 1983* (Washington D.C., 1984), 5–9.

69. Gil Loescher and John A. Scanlan, *Calculated Kindness: Refugees and America's Half-Open Door, 1945 to Present* (New York, 1986).

70. Grahl-Madsen, *The Status of Refugees in International Law* (1966), 4, and idem (1972), 93–98.

71. See, for instance, David S. Wyman, *Paper Walls: America and the Refugee Crisis, 1938–41* (New York, 1985).

72. Goodwin-Gill, *The Refugee in International Law,* 71.

73. Dennis McNamara, "The Origins and Effects of 'Humane Deterrence' Policies in Southeast Asia," in Loescher and Monahan, 125.

74. An exception to this rule is Luxembourg. It has no specific laws on refugees, but it does allow migrants to apply for asylum under the provisions of the 1951 Convention. *Refugees* (March 1991): 19.

75. Arthur C. Helton, "The Detention of Refugees and Asylum-Seekers: A Misguided Threat to Refugee Protection," in Loescher and Monahan, 135–39; Johan Cels, Responses of European States to *de facto* Refugees," in Loescher and Monahan, 191–92.

76. U.S. Committee for Refugees, *Refugee Reports* (29 January 1991): 1.

77. "France: Clearing Up the Confusion," *Refugees* (March 1991): 22.

78. Roy McDowall, "Co-ordination of Refugee Policy in Europe," in Loescher and Monahan, 181.

79. League of Nations, *Official Journal* (March–April 1921): 228.

80. *UNHCR Statutes,* Art. 1.

81. League of Nations, Nansen International Office for Refugees, "Report of the Governing Body" (Geneva, 1935) [A.22.1935.XII], 23.

82. Barbara Basler, "U.N. Panel in Hong Kong Assailed on Boat People," *New York Times,* 15 January 1991.

83. See Elizabeth Ferris, "The Churches, Refugees, and Politics," in Loescher and Monahan, 159–77.

84. League of Nations, "Report to the Council of 24 March 1924 by Dr. Nansen," 387.

85. Holborn, *UNHCR,* 136.

86. *UNHCR Statute,* Art. 1.

87. League of Nations, "Report on the Work of the High Commissioner for Refugees presented by Dr. Fridtjof Nansen to the Fourth Assembly" (Geneva, 4 September 1923) [A.30.1923.XII], 18.

88. League of Nations Archives/C1105/187(N6).

89. Fred Cuny and Barry Stein, "Prospects for and Promotion of Spontaneous Repatriation," in Loescher and Monahan, 305–6.

90. Jacques Cuenod, "Development or Relief," in Loescher and Monahan, 229–35.

91. "A World of Changing Needs," *Refugees* (April 1991): 36.

92. Stephan Ladas, *The Exchange of Minorities, Bulgaria, Greece, and Turkey* (New York, 1932).

93. Cuenod, "Development or Relief," 231–32.

94. "Cause and Effect," *Refugees* (March 1990): 5.

95. High Commissioner for Refugees and Director of the ILO, "Measures in Favour of Russian, Armenian, Assyrian, Assyro-Chaldean and Turkish Refugees: Report to the Ninth Assembly" (Geneva, 1928) [A.33.1928], 11–12.

96. Julia Vadala Taft, "A Call to Action for Restructuring U.S. Refugee Policy, in *World Refugee Survey: 1989 in Review,* 9.

97. Letter from Nansen to N. Politis, 9 November 1922, Jacob S. Worm-Mueller, ed., *Fridtjof Nansen Brev,* vol. 4, 1919–25 (Oslo, 1966), 170.

98. James G. McDonald, "Letter of Resignation with an Annex" (London, 27 December 1935). A copy of the letter is reprinted in Norman Bentwich, *The Refugees from Germany, April 1933 to Dec. 1935* (London, 1936), 119–228.

99. League of Nations, "90th Session of the Council," *Official Journal* (February 1936), 126–29.

100. Quoted in Arthur D. Morse, *While Six Million Died: A Chronicle of American Apathy* (New York, 1968), 198.

101. *UNHCR Statutes,* Art. 2.

102. Aristide R. Zolberg et al., *Escape From Violence,* 258.

103. Hocke, "Beyond Humanitarianism," 10.

104. Sadako Ogata, "A Safer World," *Refugees* (March 1991): 3.

105. Jonas Widgren, "Europe and International Migration in the Future," in Loescher and Monahan, 53.

106. Ibid., 752–53.

107. Nichols, "Rubberband Humanitarianism," 195.

MARK P. GIBNEY

Foreign Policy: Ideological and Human Rights Factors

The Berlin Wall is down; the Cold War is finally over. With the stunning victory by the United Nations forces in the Persian Gulf, President George Bush has proclaimed a "new world order." Bush provides this description of the old world: "Until now, the world we've known has been a world divided—a world of barbed wire and concrete block, conflict and cold war."[1] In contrast,

> now, we can see a new world coming into view. A world in which there is the very real prospect of a new world order. In the words of Winston Churchill, a "world order" in which "the principles of justice and fair play . . . protect the weak against the strong. . . ." A world where the United Nations, freed from cold war stalemate, is poised to fulfill the historic vision of its founders. A world in which freedom and respect for human rights find a home among all nations.[2]

What has the old world wrought? To describe the old world simply as experiencing "conflict," as Bush does, is grossly to underestimate the level of human suffering that has afflicted various peoples in the world, much of it engendered by the Cold War itself. In fact, the old world was marked by ever-increasing worldwide expenditures on military hardward and equipment and, concomitant with that, unprecedented levels of violence and death. In this world, the number of civilians killed in the course of military actions continued its steady escalation, constituting one-half of the war dead in the 1950s but nearly three-fourths by the late 1980s.[3] Another consequence of this violence has been the enormous increase in the number of refugees in the world attempting to escape from it.[4] In the

JOURNAL OF POLICY HISTORY, Vol. 4, No. 1, 1992.

past decade alone, the world's refugee population has more than doubled, to approximately 15 million.[5]

Despite what is heralded as nothing short of the metamorphosis of global politics, perhaps even the "end of history," still it is not apparent that the new world order will differ dramatically from that of the old. The prospects that nations will continue to resort to violence and that countless millions either will be killed by this violence or seek to escape from it seem reasonably certain. There also is every indication that the world's refugee regime and refugee affairs more generally, the focus here, will experience very little change from what had existed previously.

Part I examines the unchanging nature of United States refugee admissions. Part II looks at a different aspect of U.S. "refugee policy," namely, U.S. foreign policy. This section provides an overview of the level of human devastation that the superpower rivalry has helped bring about. It is argued that even if the United States and the Soviet Union were no longer to engage in proxy battles as they have been for the past few decades in virtually every corner of the globe, this still will not nearly be enough to achieve a "new world order." Unfortunately, the East-West conflict either has created or perpetuated conditions that could very well bring about even greater levels of violence and displacement.[6] It is morally unacceptable for the superpowers to simply walk away from the Frankenstein world that they have in large part created.

What is needed instead is a much different kind of intervention either than what had existed in the past or than what Bush's concept of a new world order envisions. Part III presents what a "truly new world order" (for lack of a better term) can and should look like. This particular world order unequivocally recognizes that much of the violence and the related displacement in the world has international roots.[7] Under this new vision, one of the standards by which a nation is to judge its own foreign-policy pursuits (but also how it is judged by others as well) is by the human consequences of that policy. A truly new world order places severe constraints on the ability of nations to obtain the means of destruction and violence. In addition, under this new scheme nations are to confront poverty and repression in other countries: the root causes of refugee flows and the very real consequences of decades of superpower rivalry. Finally, we must begin to view the existence of refugee flows much differently than we have in the past. Refugee flows indicate that something is "wrong" in another country. They might also indicate that something is "wrong" with our own policies as well. In sum, this is what a truly new world order would look like. The penultimate question is whether the nations of the world are willing to work toward this.

U.S. Refugee Admissions: Plus ça change . . . ?

The United States will admit 131,000 refugees in fiscal year 1991. In a world where communism is in a state of collapse—and where literally hundreds of thousands of refugees are pouring out of Iraq as this is being written—what is most remarkable about the composition of these flows is how little it has changed from previous years. That is, the vast majority of refugees who will be admitted to the United States this year will continue to be from communist countries.[8] Two ethnic groups—Vietnamese and Soviets—comprise nearly three-quarters of this number. Let us consider the justification for the large-scale admission of both groups. Let us also consider what goals a refugee admission policy ought to be serving.

Vietnamese migration to the United States dates back to the fall of Saigon in 1975. Since then, approximately one million refugees have left Vietnam, the vast majority being resettled in the United States. Although not without its humanitarian component, the United States also has used these refugee flows to serve as a reminder of the shortcomings of life under the communist regime.[9] Normalized relations and attempts to bring Vietnam back into the community of nations would go far in greatly reducing this flow;[10] however, this is not a goal of the United States. In fact, not only has U.S. policy toward Vietnam helped to perpetuate the flow of refugees from this destitute country, but its attempt ultimately to "win" the Vietnam War actually has implicated the U.S. government in genocidal policies.[11]

In opposing Vietnam's policy in Cambodia, for years the United States has provided financial and military support to the two noncommunist guerrilla forces aligned (most would say subservient) to the Khmer Rouge. In the face of growing international and domestic opposition, the Bush administration finally reversed American policy in the summer of 1990.[12] Still, the lives of ordinary Cambodians worsen. One child in five dies before the age of five, and there is one doctor for every 36,000 people in a country where malaria and tuberculosis are rampant, 15 percent of tested blood carries hepatitis, and 300 amputations are performed each month because of land mines.[13] Valerie Sutter's recent study of the Indochina refugee dilemma offers little prospect for hope:

> Regrettably, this investigation concludes without insight into a magic formula for resolving this most perplexing refugee dilemma. In fact, the potential for increases in the tragic elements of this ongoing saga appear all too evident in the precarious Cambodian situation and in the continuing isolation of Indochina, which keeps those states chron-

ically underdeveloped. There have been increases in the exodus, a deterioration of first asylum, proclivity toward abusing refugees who seek asylum, and a decline in resettlement opportunities. Perhaps of the greatest concern now are complacency regarding the status quo and a waning interest in the Indochina refugee issue altogether.[14]

Rather than pursuing policies that would diminish the prospects of violence and help stem the flow of refugees from Southeast Asia, the U.S. government has long taken the opposite approach. The admission of 50,000 Vietnamese refugees this year, and, most likely, in the foreseeable future as well, should not be viewed as a humanitarian gesture. Instead, it should be seen as a belated—and very inadequate—response to a foreign policy that has helped to produce substantial numbers of refugees in the past and that will continue to do so in the future. As Terry Anderson has written of U.S. policy: "Isolation, really, is a hiatus from reality; it is an excuse for no policy, an attempt to wish our problems away in Southeast Asia. Those problems will not disappear magically, and, in fact, isolation has had little positive impact on the MIA issue or the Kampuchean imbroglio."[15]

What *should* U.S. policy look like? The United States should normalize relations with Vietnam immediately and seek to work through the United Nations to avert another bloodbath in Cambodia. Rather than interpreting refugee flows from Vietnam as a victory for our side, as we have done in the past, such flows should be viewed as a shortcoming of our foreign policy in that area. Much has been made about the recent Persian Gulf war removing the albatross of Vietnam. Unfortunately, this so-called albatross involves only military might and will. What should be hanging from our national consciousness is the plight of the Vietnamese people, as evidenced by the continual flow of refugees and the fact that this nation's gross national product is now one of the lowest in the world.

Much like Vietnamese refugee flows, the admission of approximately 50,000 Soviets this year is also a continuation of past policy. Both migrations have been driven by foreign-policy considerations. Both migrations have only served to exacerbate problems within those countries. Finally, both migrations should be halted and U.S. refugee admission policy reevaluated.

This is not the place to begin to describe the long-standing efforts by the United States to admit Soviet refugees.[16] Suffice it to say that in one form or another, and with varying levels of success, this has been an overriding goal of U.S. foreign policy over the past few decades.[17] For some time, both the United States and Israel have denounced the Soviet Union for severely restricting the right to emigrate. Soviet policy changed dramatically in the late 1980s. The U.S. response has been less certain. Faced with the prospect of unprecedented levels of Soviet emigration, in 1989 the State Department reversed a long-standing policy of the United States government by placing a limit on the number of Soviet refugees that could be admitted to this country.[18]

Where will U.S. policy go from here? The most likely prospect is a muddled policy where the numbers from the past two years, approximately 50,000, will become the accepted norm. This, however, will accomplish very little, and it will most certainly weaken the already precarious economic conditions that currently exist in the Soviet Union.[19] There are literally millions of people who wish to leave the Soviet Union. At some point soon the absorptive capacity of Israel will be reached. The possibility of resettling large numbers of Soviets in the West are not good either.[20] The admission of 50,000 Soviet "refugees" gives the appearance of responding to a crisis, but what it does instead is to avoid facing the much more difficult question of how to assist in restructuring Soviet society so that people do not want to leave.

In addition to being bad public policy, the admission of large numbers of Vietnamese and Soviets also raises an issue of fairness. Despite passage of the 1980 Refugee Act and the purported concern with the "plight of the refugee," there has been a long-standing divorce between the level of human rights violations in other countries and the refugee/asylum response of the U.S. government.[21] The vast majority of Soviets and Vietnamese do not have a "well-founded fear of persecution." As a result, they should not be granted refugee status. In doing so, we deprive other, more deserving individuals an opportunity for resettlement in this country. What sums up the poverty of U.S. refugee policy is that at the same time we are admitting tens of thousands of Soviets and Vietnamese, we are not offering any resettlement to the hundreds of thousands of refugees flooding out of Iraq. There is something drastically wrong with this state of affairs. There is something drastically wrong with a refugee policy that provides no assistance to people who are fleeing for their lives but, at the same time, gives resettlement assistance to people who simply want to join their relatives or make a new start in life.

The Pursuit of Foreign-Policy Objectives and the Creation of Refugee Flows

Until recently, most scholars have ignored the international causes of refugee flows. Instead, as Aristide Zolberg, Astri Suhrke, and Sergio

Aguayo have explained, what has long dominated the refugee literature is what they have termed an "internalist" perspective:

> The international dimension of the causes of refugee movements has not been recognized in prevailing legal concepts and definitions. . . . [F]actors internal to the country of origin predominate in conventional interpretations of persecution. An internalist emphasis also has influenced public perceptions of the origins of refugee movements. This not only is incorrect but also obscures the point that external parties by action—or inaction—can significantly influence the processes that generate refugees. Refugees do not appear simply because they are persecuted by government X or victimized by brutalizing rulers in weak states; such governments and states exist within a necessary structure of international support. It follows that outside parties and humanitarian groups concerned with refugees must make foreign policy a matter of abiding concern.[22]

In the previous section it was argued that the pursuit of U.S. foreign-policy objectives in Southeast Asia has been a major factor in perpetuating the flow of refugees from Vietnam and elsewhere in the region. It also was argued that the United States could pursue different policies that would not have these same human consequences, and that a "truly new world order" would dictate as such. We now turn to other areas of the world that have served as scenes for proxy battles between the East and the West, and where the human devastation has been staggering. With the passing of the old order and the proclamation of a new one, the question that needs to be addressed is what this will mean—or should mean—in terms of how the two superpowers, and the West more generally, will conduct their foreign affairs. In particular, will the advent of a "new world order" be interpreted by both the Soviet Union and the United States as a license to walk away from the devastation they have done so much to create but which will continue to afflict the peoples of the Third World for some time to come?

Latin America

The World Bank has termed the last ten years "The Lost Decade" for Latin America.[23] The continuing civil war in El Salvador already has brought about the deaths of more than 75,000 civilians and the displacement of another 1.5 million people. The war between the U.S.-backed contra rebel forces and the ruling Sandinista regime in Nicaragua resulted in the deaths of approximately 30,000 civilians and the displacement of another half-million individuals. In Guatemala, statewide terror first began after the CIA directed the murder of President Arbenz in 1954. Since that time more than 100,000 civilians have been killed by the military, most in the past decade. In addition, approximately 1.5 million of Guatemala's eight million people have fled the country since 1978.[24] While the political violence in Honduras has not reached anywhere near these levels, for much of the past decade this country's sovereignty has been ceded to the United States, which has turned the country into something akin to a U.S. military base, or "America's whore."[25]

In tandem with these unprecedented levels of violence, poverty also has increased markedly throughout the region. At present, for example, nine in ten Guatemalan families live in poverty, and those suffering from abject poverty—defined as those unable to feed themselves—jumped from one in eight to one in three during the decade.[26]

The United States has been very active in pursuing certain foreign-policy objectives in Latin America throughout the past decade. To policy-makers in the Reagan administration what was at stake was nothing less than the balance of global power.[27] Given the enormous importance attributed to this region, however, do not presume that American policy-makers necessarily had (or have) an inherent interest in peace and the well-being of those who live in Latin America. Instead, as Lars Schoultz has argued: "Few U.S. policy makers would be concerned if Salvadorans or Guatemalans or Haitians spent their time shooting one another were it not for the fact that one possible consequence of this instability might be to provide hostile forces with the opportunity to seize territory in Latin America and then use it to threaten U.S. security."[28]

Yet, despite U.S. policy over the past decade—arguably as a very real consequence of it—Guatemalans shot at Guatemalans, Nicaraguans shot at Nicaraguans, Salvadorans shot at Salvadorans, and so on, all with the aim of halting the perceived spread of Soviet influence in Latin America and elsewhere. Assuming, then, that this rationale can no longer be employed, and that Central America will no longer serve as a grounds for a proxy battle between the two superpowers, will this region of the globe now be transformed? Nora Hamilton and Norma Chinchilla recently have suggested that even if the fighting in Latin America were to cease soon, the underlying causes of violence and displacement will remain.

> What distinguishes the massive population movements in Central America today from those of the past is the conjuncture of several factors: an economic crisis, a consequence of the changes in the capitalist world economy and their specific forms in each Central

American country, combined with political conflict arising from the growing contradictions between capitalist modernization and the backward socioeconomic structures maintained over time by the repressive state apparatus. U.S. involvement in these conflicts has prolonged and intensified them without resolving the structural contradictions from which they emerged. Prolonging the conflicts has in turn aggravated the economic crisis, which cannot be expected to disappear once the conflicts end. Thus one effect that can be anticipated is the continued dislocation, displacement, and migration of substantial sectors of the Central American populations.[29]

Does the "new world order" mean that the United States will devote as much effort and money in fighting against *these* evils as it did in its fight against perceived communist expansion? The prospects are not encouraging. Fighting insurgency is much easier than fighting the underlying causes for the insurgency. Fighting an insurgency labeled as "communist" has made the fighting, or the support of others' fighting, that much easier. President Bush has described a "new world order" as one in which the "principles of justice and fair play . . . protect the weak against the strong." However, when Bush is speaking about the "strong," he is simply referring to external sources of aggression, such as Iraq's invasion of Kuwait. Bush's very slow and inadequate response to the situation facing the Kurdish rebels after the Persian Gulf war indicates that if the "strong" are an internal force, as they are in Latin America and elsewhere, the "weak" cannot expect assistance from the United States.

There is little hope, then, that the United States will begin to address the underlying causes of violence and displacement in Latin America. What might possibly change this is the fact that, unlike other refugee-producing areas of the world, geographic proximity might not give the United States the opportunity to ignore the dire situation facing most of Central America. The specter of "feet people" migrating to the United States, employed so frequently by the Reagan administration in order to obtain support for its policy in this region,[30] is still likely to occur in the future, despite strenuous efforts to seal the southern border. Such a human tidal wave may well be the only means of grabbing the attention of the American public and of U.S. policymakers, but even this much is not certain.

Africa

Fifteen million people on the African continent have been uprooted from their homes, half from violence and conflict, and the rest in search of food. With rare exception, this human tragedy is removed from the Western conscience. Consider, for example, the small number of African refugees resettled in the United States. Yet refugee flows from both the Horn of Africa and the Southern Cone can be tied directly to the superpower rivalry over the past few decades.[31]

One of the largest refugee-producing countries in southern Africa is Angola. Since the start of civil war in the 1970s, both the United States and the Soviet Union have pursued their own foreign-policy objectives in this country through the use of proxies. The U.S. has supported the National Union for the Total Independence of Angola (UNITA) rebel forces and the South African military. The Soviets have backed the People's Movement for the Liberation of Angola (MPLA) and the presence of Cuban military personnel. In 1976 the U.S. Congress passed the Clark Amendment, which prohibited further military assistance for antigovernment forces in Angola. At the same time, South Africa began to reduce its own support for UNITA. However, in late 1979 and 1980 the South African military once again moved into Angola. Coinciding with these events was the election of Ronald Reagan, a staunch supporter of UNITA. What ensued during the past decade were enormously high levels of violence and the creation of large-scale refugee flows. In terms of the latter, Schultheis estimates that half a million or more Angolans have found refuge in Zaire and another 150,000 in Zambia.[32]

Mozambique experienced a similar hell this past decade, one in which nearly one million Mozambicans fled into neighboring countries. In addition, hundreds of thousands of individuals are internal refugees, and the vast majority face starvation.[33] South Africa's attempt to destabilize neighboring regimes is well documented, in the case of Mozambique through its support for the Mozambique National Resistance.[34] What is not as well known is that both the Soviet Union and the United States also have played an important role in the origin and the perpetuation of this conflict.[35]

Tragedy has now become synonymous with the Horn of Africa. The endless cycle of fighting and famine has killed or displaced hundreds of thousands of people. Once again, both the Soviet Union and the United States have been actively involved in this region for decades, both countries having backed several different factions in the litany of disputes involving the conflict between Ethiopia and Somalia, the Eritrean and Tigrean independence movements in Ethiopia, and Somalia's own civil war.[36]

What are the prospects for the future? The situation in Mozambique continues to look bleak, as violence and refugee flows continued unabated during 1990.[37] The drastically reduced tension between the Soviet Union and the United States, however, in addition to the start of the process of dismantling apartheid in South Africa, has led to encouraging prospects for peace in Angola.[38] In the Horn of Africa, much of the current round of fighting appears to be over, brought about in large part by an agreement between the superpowers not to intervene. What is left, however, is devastation and the real possibility that new fighting will break out again. Jane Perlez filed this report on the aftermath of civil war in Somalia: "Amid the debris of its civil war, Somalia is struggling to start anew. But this sliver of a country on the Horn of Africa, once regarded as a strategic prize for the superpowers and now nearly forgotten, has little to work with other than the legacy of expensive and lethal cold-war weapons that helped propel its war."[39]

Despite some measure for optimism in the short run, the long-range prospects in Africa are numbing. Twenty-three of the world's thirty poorest countries are in sub-Saharan Africa, and the average annual income in those countries is below $220.[40] The World Bank projects that by the end of the decade this part of the continent will account for more than 30 percent of the developing world's poor, as against 16 percent in 1985.[41] Added to this, most areas in Africa face grave ecological disaster. The continent is losing forests at the rate of 1.3 million hectares a year. In sub-Saharan Africa nearly seven million kilometers of land, an area twice the size of India, are under direct threat of decertification. The situation in the Horn of Africa is just as bleak, if not bleaker, as one famine in that region begins to blend with all the previous ones, and where upward of 27 million people are currently at serious risk of starvation.

While some of the current fighting on the African continent might cease, there is no assurance that this ultimately will bring a halt to violence and displacement. In fact, given the demographic and ecological projections, just the opposite can be said with far more assurance. This raises the same question asked before: Does the "new world order" mean nothing more than that the United States and the Soviet Union will agree not to intervene in Africa as they have done for the past few decades? The answer to this question seems to be yes. What this will leave in place, most assuredly, are situations that promise to bring about levels of violence and related refugee flows that will be just as devastating as what we have witnessed in the past. But, then again, the West really has never witnessed these flows in the first place.

Afghanistan

No country has produced more refugees in the past decade than Afghanistan. Since the Soviet invasion in 1979, between five and six million people—more than a third of the country's population—have fled to Pakistan or Iran. This toll is in addition to the 1.3 million Afghanis who were killed in the course of the war itself.[42] The overwhelming blame for this human carnage of course lies directly with the Soviet Union. However, the U.S.-backed forces share at least part of the blame for some of the atrocities that occurred during the war, and for the continuing violence subsequent to the Soviet withdrawal.[43]

Afghanistan epitomizes the shortcomings of the so-called new world order. While an apparent consensus now exists between the Soviet Union and the United States not to intervene in the affairs of this country[44] (or at least not to intervene to the same extent as they had), there has been no attempt to put this war-ravaged country back together. In this respect, the Vietnam analogy is an apt one. Predictably, Afghanistan will become the forgotten country, vitally important at one time to the superpowers when it served their ideological purposes, cast aside when this too was in their perceived national interests.

The Persian Gulf

The euphoria proclaiming a new world order has been prompted in large part by the swift victory of the U.S.-led Allied forces in the Persian Gulf. The reason for the euphoria is really simple to explain: Allied casualties were nearly nonexistent. Essentially ignored in the West is the fact that upward of 100,000 Iraqi soldiers and untold numbers of Iraqi civilians were killed during the war itself. Many more people will die as the result of civil strife and the fact that Iraq has been bombed back into a "pre-industrial society."[45] Finally, the war and its aftermath (which has been more war) has produced one of the largest refugee flows in history.[46]

As I will argue in the next section, one of the most important principles that ought to guide a nation in the conduct of its foreign policy are the human consequences of that policy. Ironically enough, given these levels of human devastation, it was exactly this kind of rationale that was used in the decision to employ force in the Persian Gulf in the first place. It is not clear what one should conclude from this. One conclusion might be that the goals of the Allied forces were well intentioned but not farsighted enough to realize the kind of terror and turmoil that would ensue. Or one might conclude what I suggested here: that the new world order, unfortunately, looks remarkably like the old one.

A Truly New World Order

One of the hallmarks of the old world order was that nations (but really only powerful nations) pursued their foreign-policy objectives with little, if any, concern to the human consequences that would flow from those pursuits. What this has helped bring about is human devastation. There are two reasons why nations feel immune to the consequences of their actions—one moral and the other practical.

Until recently, scholars have not placed the creation of refugees into a larger international context. The reason for this goes much deeper than simply misunderstanding the root causes of refugee flows. Instead, it is a clear indication that Western scholars, and policymakers, have not given much consideration to the relationship that exists (and that ought to exist) between one nation and citizens of other countries. Lea Brilmayer has pointed out that while international relations theory has been concerned with relations between states (what she refers to as the "horizontal" relationship), and while political theory focuses on the relationship between the state and citizens of the same state (the "vertical"), what has been ignored is the "diagonal" relationship that exists between a nation that is pursuing certain foreign-policy objectives and citizens of other countries where those pursuits are having an effect.

As a result of this dichotomy, vastly different moral standards are applied depending on whether one is acting in the domestic or the international domain. What occurs all too frequently, Brilmayer argues, is that there are certain standards by which a nation treats its own and a completely different set of standards (or, more likely, no standards at all) in our dealings with individuals in other countries. Brilmayer registers her objection in the form of a question: "Is there any way to explain why an action suddenly becomes legitimate when it is undertaken outside one's territory? Would support for death squads in El Salvador be any different from support for death squads in Miami?"[47]

More than two decades ago William Fulbright commented on the divorce between international and domestic morality. Although he was criticizing U.S. policy in Vietnam, his analysis goes well beyond this one example:

> Man's capacity for decent behavior seems to vary directly with his perceptions of others as individual humans with human motives and feelings, whereas his capacity for barbarous behavior seems to increase with his perception of an adversary in abstract terms. This is the only explanation I can think of for the fact that the very same

good and decent citizens who would never fail to feed a hungry child
or comfort a sick friend or drop a coin in the church basket can
celebrate the number of Viet Cong killed in a particular week or
battle, talking of "making a desert" of North Vietnam or of "bombing
it back to the Stone Age" despite the fact that most, almost all, of
the victims would be innocent peasants and workers.[48]

The second reason why we allow ourselves to treat foreign nationals
differently than how we treat our own is a practical reason that follows
from the moral reason, but it is even more basic and perhaps more telling.
Simply put, we treat individuals in other countries differently than we
treat our own because we can get away with doing so. This is not to say
that we intend to harm others. In fact, our intentions are often quite
benevolent. However, in the course of attempting to help, we often cause
far more harm. We seem incapable of comprehending this fact; a point
that is underscored by the Persian Gulf victory party in the United States
at the same time that people are being massacred in Iraq in the aftermath
of the war. One reason why we seem so incapable of understanding the
harm that we have caused others is that we have never been held accountable for it. An example of this phenomenon is the quick dismissal of
lawsuits brought in American courts by foreign plaintiffs alleging human
rights violations by the U.S. government.[49]

The most essential aspect of achieving a truly new world order is to
change drastically the way that we think of people in other societies.
Robert Holmes has suggested that

> what is needed is a new perspective that sees the people of the world
> as arrayed, not basically against one another, but against the deceit,
> ignorance, and arrogance of governments and the ways of thinking
> that have produced them. What is needed is a new respect for the
> preciousness and inviolability of the human person. This does not
> require changing human nature or transforming the world into a
> community of saints. It does require recognizing that if we do not
> cherish the human person, there is no point to many other activities
> and strivings that consume our time; no point to saving the environ-
> ment unless we value the beings that inhabit it; no virtue in self-
> sacrifice when it is at the expense and lives of others.[50]

What follows are principles that nations ought to abide by in an attempt to reverse the levels of violence and displacement in the world.
While these might appear to be utopian to some, they are no more

utopian than the proclamation of a new world order. These principles also might appear to be based simply on notions of charity and goodwill. This is not the case. Instead, they are premised on a notion of compensatory justice that recognizes that the global powers have pursued policies that have helped cause enormous levels of human devastation and suffering to other people.

1. Recognize the International Causes of Refugee Flows

While refugee scholars have been slow in recognizing the international context in which most refugee flows occur, policymakers still have not done so. A vital first step, then, is a public recognition by both the Soviet government and the U.S. government that their deadly rivalry has contributed heavily to the vast levels of violence and displacement that now afflict the Third World. In many respects it is surprising that Third World governments have not already demanded this.

In the past few years there have been an unprecedented number of instances where nations have publicly apologized or at least recognized the human rights violations that they (usually a predecessor government) have committed: the Japanese internment during World War II; the complicity in crimes committed by East European countries;[51] the state-sponsored terrorism in such countries as Uraguay, Chile, Brazil, and Argentina, and so on.[52] I suggest a similar kind of acknowledgment. Before we can begin constructing a new world order, we must first recognize our own role (and the Soviets should do the same) in creating the devastating conditions of the old world.

2. Judge Foreign-Policy Pursuits by Their Human Consequences

It is difficult to say in the abstract what is good or bad foreign policy. We do have some criteria by which to judge domestic policy, the most basic being a utilitarian-type calculation under which policies that harm our citizens ought to be avoided and those that aid or assist them should be adopted. These same kinds of principles ought to be followed in the international realm as well. Nations should be able to pursue policies that they perceive to be in their own national interest, but they no longer should be able to do so at the expense of others. One vital criterion that ought to be employed to judge a nation's foreign policy is the human consequences that flow from it. Policies that harm people ought to be avoided; those that assist people (all people, not just our own citizens) ought to be pursued. During the Cold War, Western nations always could rationalize their foreign policy objectives, no matter what level of human devastation ensued from those policies, on the basis that this ultimately was a better result than what Communism would bring.[53] One can presume that policymakers in the East made the same kind of argument. This rationalization can no longer be employed. Thus, nations should seek to avoid causing harm to individuals in other societies, and, moreover, they ought to be held accountable when they do so.

3. Place Restraints on Obtaining the Means of Violence

If the Persian Gulf war seemed to teach any lesson, it was this: the indiscriminate sale of military weapons ultimately can (perhaps will) cause disastrous human consequences. Yet in the immediate aftermath of the war this lesson has been ignored. Instead of attempting to de-escalate the probability of mass destruction in the Middle East, nations from all over the globe have used this opportunity to re-arm the countries in this volatile region.[54] The problem, unfortunately, goes well beyond the Middle East. As Jonas Widgren has pointed out, arms expenditures are twenty-five times greater than the amounts spent on official assistance. He continues: "Arms consume money which, if invested in social, educational, and other civil fields would contribute to a better way of life for millions of people, thus lessening the strains and tensions in society that cause migratory flows and—ultimately—threaten the peace of the world."[55]

How, then, does one explain the continuing world arms bazaar? Much like foreign intervention (in fact, even more so), nations that sell military hardware to other countries do so at no cost to *themselves* in human terms. In fact, quite the opposite is true. There will be instances, of course, where the purchaser of weapons will use these weapons against the seller—certainly this happened during the Persian Gulf war—but these situations are few and far between. The more usual pattern is for the purchaser to sell, turn a profit, and watch from afar as these weapons are used against other people. This would not happen if those who sold military hardware were implicated in the destruction and devastation these weapons brought about. This is what a new world order demands.

4. Fight Poverty and Repression

The principles discussed thus far relate to foreign intervention, whether in the form of direct military intervention or in the more indirect forms such as the sale of weapons to the Third World. However, it is *not* being suggested that under a truly new world order nations should stop intervening in the affairs of other countries. Foreign intervention already has occurred and the results have been disastrous. To walk away from this devastation would simply be yet another means of pursuing our own short-term self-interest, notwithstanding the human costs to others. What is needed instead is a much different kind of intervention.

One area where we can immediately begin this new form of intervention is in our foreign aid program. Our present system is a travesty. Security assistance now comprises two-thirds of U.S. foreign aid, and it also is the fasting-growing part.[56] The driving force behind American foreign assistance, it almost goes without saying, has been to contain Communist domination. This threat, if it ever was a threat, is over. Yet this metamorphosis has not prompted any perceptible change in U.S. policy, or even an apparent attempt to reevaluate U.S. foreign assistance. What is needed is a foreign assistance program that attempts to meet the basic rights of other peoples.[57] We have not had such a program.

5. Reinterpret Refugee Flows

We now have a unique opportunity to reverse long-standing policies that have led to large-scale violence and displacement in the world. The passing of the East-West conflict should dictate a complete reexamination of our relationship with the Third World. It should force us to recognize the degree to which we are responsible for so much of the human devastation that exists in these countries. It also should force us to develop, and pursue, vastly different policies than we have under the old world order.

Refugee flows are symptoms that something is "wrong": wrong in the country producing refugees, but wrong in the foreign policies of other countries as well. This is not to say that refugee flows should be avoided at all costs. Instead, to do so "would be the equivalent of trying to oppose social change."[58] What this does mean, however, is that we must end the exilic bias that exists in refugee affairs.[59] What this has done has been to allow ourselves to avoid addressing the root causes of refugee flows, including our own role in the creation or perpetuation of such populations. Our ultimate goal should be to construct a new and far different relationship between nations and between citizens of other countries. This is indeed a daunting task, but, then again, we have been promised a new world order.

Purdue University

Notes

1. George Bush, "Address to Congress on End of Gulf War," *New York Times*, 7 March 1991.

2. Ibid.

3. Ruth Leger Sivard, *World Military and Social Expenditures* (Washington, D.C., 1989), 11.

4. Aristide Zolberg, Astri Suhrke, and Sergio Aguayo, *Escape From Violence: Conflict and the Refugee Crisis in the Developing World* (New York, 1989).

5. United Nations High Commissioner for Refugees, *Refugees* (December 1990).

6. Aristide Zolberg, "The New Waves: Migration Theory for a Changing World," *International Migration Review* 23 (1989): 403.

7. Gil Loescher, "Introduction," in Gil Loescher and Laila Monahan, eds., *Refugees and International Relations* (New York, 1989); Zolberg et al., *Escape From Violence*.

8. Gil Loescher and John Scanlan, *Calculated Kindness: Refugees and America's Half-Open Door, 1945 to the Present* (New York, 1986); Norm Zucker and Naomi Flink Zucker, *The Guarded Gate: The Reality of American Refugee Policy* (New York, 1987).

9. Michael Teitelbaum, "Immigration, Refugees and Foreign Policy," *International Organizations* 38 (1984): 429.

10. Binh Le and Mark Gibney, "U.S. Foreign Policy and Vietnamese Refugee Flows," *International Third World Studies Journal & Review* (forthcoming).

11. Paul Kattenburg, "Living with Hanoi," *Foreign Policy* (Winter 1983/84): 131.

12. Thomas Friedman, "U.S. Shifts Cambodia Policy; Ends Recognition of Rebels; Agrees to Talks with Hanoi," *New York Times*, 19 July 1990.

13. Steven Erlanger, "No Haven from Agony for Cambodians," *New York Times*, 2 May 1991.

14. Valerie O'Connor Sutter, *The Indochinese Refugee Dilemma* (Baton Rouge, 1990), 224.

15. Terry H. Anderson, "The Light at the End of the Tunnel: The United States and the Socialist Republic of Vietnam," *Diplomatic History* 12 (1984): 457.

16. Paula Stern, *Water's Edge: Domestic Politics and the Making of American Foreign Policy* (New York, 1979).

17. Laurie Salitan, "Domestic Pressures and the Politics of Exit: Trends in Soviet Emigration Policy," *Political Science Quarterly* 104 (1989–90): 671.

18. Robert Pear, "U.S. Drafts Plans to Curb Admission of Soviet Jews," *New York Times*, 3 September 1990.

19. Carey Goldberg, "Tidal Wave of Emigration Carries Off Soviet 'Brains,' " *Los Angeles Times*, 8 October 1990.

20. Leon Aron, "The Russians Are Coming," *Washington Post*, 27 January 1991.

21. Mark Gibney, "A 'Well-Founded Fear' of Persecution," *Human Rights Quarterly* 10 (1988): 109; Mark Gibney and Michael Stohl, "Human Rights and U.S. Refugee Policy," in Mark Gibney, ed., *Open Borders? Closed Societies?: The Ethical and Political Issues* (Westport, Conn., 1988).

22. Zolberg et al., *Escape From Violence*, 264.

23. World Bank, "Poverty: World Development Indicators" (New York, 1990).

24. Beatriz Manz, *Refugees of a Hidden War: The Aftermath of Counterinsurgency in Guatemala* (Albany, N.Y., 1988).

25. Lars Schoultz, *National Security and the United States Policy Toward Latin America* (Princeton, 1987).

26. Linda Gruson, "Remembering a Tortured Child Who Lived in the Streets of Guatemala City," *New York Times*, 14 October 1990.

27. Schoultz, *National Security and the United States Policy Toward Latin America*, 270.

28. Ibid., 38.

29. Nora Hamilton and Norma Stolz Chinchilla, "Central American Migration: A Framework for Analysis," *Latin American Research Review* 26 (1991): 106.

30. Schoultz, *National Security and the United States Policy Toward Latin America*, 228–29.

31. Michael Schultheis, "Refugees in Africa: The Geopolitics of Forced Displacement," *African Studies Review* 32 (1989): 4; Zaki Laidi, *The Superpowers in Africa: The Constraints of a Rivalry, 1960–1990* (Chicago, 1990).

32. Schultheis, "Refugees in Africa," 5.

33. Ibid.

34. Keith Somerville, *Foreign Military Intervention in Africa* (New York, 1990).

35. Joseph Hanlon, *Beggar Your Neighbours: Apartheid Power in Southern Africa* (London, 1986); Phyllis Johnson and David Martin, ed., *Destructive Engagement: Southern Africa at War* (Harare, 1986).

36. Robert Patman, *The Soviet Union in the Horn of Africa: The Diplomacy of Intervention and Disengagement* (Cambridge, 1990).

37. United Nations High Commissioner for Refugees, 1990.

38. Alan Riding, "Angola in Accord With Guerrillas on a Cease-Fire," *New York Times,* 2 May 1991.

39. Jane Perlez, "Two Months After Ousting Despot, Somalia Faces Life as an Abandoned Pawn," *New York Times,* 4 April 1991.

40. Schultheis, "Refugees in Africa," 11.

41. World Bank, "Poverty: World Development Indicators," 5.

42. Barnett R. Rubin, "The Fragmentation of Afghanistan," *Foreign Affairs* (Winter 1989): 150.

43. John F. Burns, "Afghans: Now They Blame America," *New York Times Magazine,* 4 February 1990.

44. Elaine Sciolino, "U.S. May be Ready to End Assistance to Afghan Rebels," *New York Times,* 12 May 1991.

45. United Nations, "Report on Need for Humanitarian Assistance in Iraq" [excerpts in *New York Times,* 23 March 1991].

46. Clyde Haberman, "The Plight of the Kurds Worsens as Relief Efforts Still Fall Short," *New York Times,* 16 April 1991.

47. Lea Brilmayer, *Justifying International Acts* (Ithaca, N.Y., 1989).

48. William Fulbright, *The Arrogance of Power* (New York, 1966), 165.

49. Mark Gibney, "Human Rights and Human Consequences: A Critical Examination of *Sanchez-Espinoza v. Reagan,*" *Loyola of Los Angeles International and Comparative Law Review* 10 (1988): 299; Mark Gibney, ed., *World Justice? U.S. Courts and International Human Rights* (Boulder, Colo., 1991).

50. Robert Holmes, *On Law and Morality* (Princeton, 1989), 291.

51. Celestine Bohlen, "Hungarians Debate How Far Back to Go to Right Old Wrongs," *New York Times,* 15 April 1990.

52. Iain Guest, *Behind the Disappearances: Argentina's Dirty War Against Human Rights and the United Nations* (Philadelphia, 1990); Lawrence Weschler, *A Miracle, A Universe: Settling Accounts with Torturers* (New York, 1990).

53. Schoultz, *National Security and the United States Policy Toward Latin America.*

54. Charles Lane, "Arms for Sale," *Newsweek,* 8 April 1991.

55. Jonas Widgren, "Europe and International Migration in the Future: The Necessity of Merging Migration, Refugee, and Development Policies," in Loescher and Monahan, ed., 58.

56. Frances Moore Lappe, Rachel Schurman, and Kevin Danaher, *Betraying the National Interest* (New York, 1987), 9.

57. Henry Shue, *Basic Rights: Subsistence, Affluence and U.S. Foreign Policy* (Princeton, 1980).

58. Zolberg et al., *Escape From Violence,* 262.

59. Gervase Coles, "Approaching the Refugee Problem Today," in Loescher and Monahan, ed.; James Hathaway, "A Reconsideration of the Underlying Premise of Refugee Law," *Harvard International Law Journal* 31 (1990): 129.

NORMAN L. ZUCKER
NAOMI FLINK ZUCKER

From Immigration to Refugee Redefinition: A History of Refugee and Asylum Policy in the United States

Refugee policy in the United States is a recent offspring of American immigration policy. Like its parent, refugee admissions are firmly entangled in the thicket of national politics and are Janus-faced. One face presses for admission, the other urges restriction. While the gates of admission are always guarded, time and circumstance determine which face prevails.

American immigration, refugee, and asylum policy, while intertwined statutorily and politically, nonetheless may be separated into five distinct periods. In the first and longest period, the era of immigration, no legal distinction was made between an immigrant and a refugee. The second period, the era of fear, began with Hitler's rise to power and lasted through the end of World War II. During the third period, the era of conscience, which lasted from the end of World War II through the 1970s, refugees were admitted as refugees, under special ad hoc legislation, the refugee provisions of the 1952 Immigration and Naturalization Act, or the attorney general's parole authority. The fourth period, the era of legal obligation, was the decade of the 1980s, when refugees and asylees were admitted under the provisions of the watershed Refugee Act of 1980. Finally, during the present period, the era of redefinition, policymakers are being forced to reassess the 1980 act in light of the radical new political realities in the world and the persistence of the global refugee problem.

In the first period, the era of immigration, which extended from the beginning of the republic until the rise of Hitler, United States law made no distinction between an immigrant and a refugee and the concept of asylum had no statutory basis. Waves of newcomers arrived on America's

JOURNAL OF POLICY HISTORY, Vol. 4, No. 1, 1992.
Copyright © 1992 The Pennsylvania State University, University Park, PA.

shores, some pulled by prospects of a better life, others pushed by poverty, religious intolerance, demeaning class distinctions, and political upheavals. Today, those fleeing the revolutions of 1848 might easily be classified as refugees. For others who fled the tandem blights of poverty and systematic religious persecution, it would be debated whether they were "economic" or "political" refugees. Throughout this period, restrictionists grumbled, but it was not until 1875 that Congress passed the first federal limits on immigration, prohibiting the importation of prostitutes and alien convicts.[1]

Given the climate of the times, it was a short step from the reasonable exclusion of undesirables to the exclusion of Chinese in 1882 and the formation of the Immigration Restriction League in 1894. The league attained its objectives with the enactment of exclusionary legislation in the 1920s. Ironically, as America was closing its gates, the plight of refugees in Europe was rising to a crisis.

Refugees arose from the Soviet Revolution and subsequent counterrevolutions and from the Turkish persecution of Armenians. Still more refugees were created in the bleak depression decade of the 1930s. But it was Adolph Hitler's ascension to total power in Germany, impelling a flood of Jewish and antifascist refugees, that created the second period. The *Anschluss*, the annexation of the Sudetenland, the occupation of Czechoslovakia, and the invasion of Poland and the start of World War II swelled the refugee stream. The era of fear had begun.

In Congress, from 1933 through 1938, refugee advocates introduced a variety of bills to help German refugees. None passed. One bill proposed to admit refugees outside the limitations of the immigration quota. Another bill proposed that the unused quota allotments be made available to refugees. Still another bill would have had President Franklin D. Roosevelt widen quotas for refugees and exempt unaccompanied minors and refugees sponsored by organizations from the "likely to be a public charge" provision of the immigration law. The United States still refused to distinguish between immigrants seeking opportunity and refugees fleeing persecution. The restrictionists stood firm and dominated policy, which responded to the refugee crisis by creating barriers to entrance. Neither these nor other refugee relief measures received much attention. The only legislation to gain serious consideration was the Wagner-Rogers bill, which gave rise to the quintessential confrontation between the restrictionists and the admissionists.

The Wagner-Rogers bill proposed the admission of twenty thousand German refugee children under the age of fourteen on a nonquota basis over a two-year period (ten thousand in 1939 and ten thousand in 1940).

To avoid provoking anti-Semitism, the bill was deliberately termed a German rather than a Jewish refugee children's bill, while the public committee created to support the bill was carefully called the Non-Sectarian Committee for German Refugee Children. While there was an amazing outpouring of humanitarian support for the bill, it could not surmount the wall of nativist resistance. The restrictionists feared that any opening of the gates would countervail the restrictive legislation of the twenties. (The bill failed. Despite the nonsectarian cast of its title, most people perceived the modest bill as intended for the rescue of Jewish children. One year later, Congress, with alacrity, passed a measure to allow the entrance of British children.)

Official Washington had followed, or perhaps had shaped, public opinion. The Department of State opposed the children's bill. The Labor Department waffled, neither supporting nor opposing it. Franklin D. Roosevelt, in the White House, took the politically expedient course of silence. No less than the Congress, the executive branch moved to impede refugee entrance. The Congress did so by failing to remove restrictive barriers. The executive constructed, in historian David S. Wyman's felicitous term, "paper walls."[2] After the war began, the State Department restrained the intake of refugees by imposing stricter administrative requirements. Affidavits of financial support were no longer accepted from relatives, and evidence of paid ship passage was required. On the pretense that the Nazis were infiltrating the refugee flow, the State Department instructed its overseas processing staff to withhold visas from anyone about whom they had doubts.

During the critical years from 1940 to 1944, Assistant Secretary of State Breckenridge Long was primarily responsible for refugee matters. Long was by temperament and philosophy a restrictionist. Under him the State Department piled regulation upon regulation. A "relatives rule" stipulated that any visa applicant with a close relative remaining in German, Italian, or Russian territory had to pass a security test. A subsequent broadening of this rule required that all immigration applications undergo a security review by a special interdepartmental committee. Papers moved with painstaking delay through the screening bureaucracy. By July 1943 the visa application form was more than four feet long and had to be filled out on both sides and submitted in sextuplicate. After 1941, consuls were given unlimited authority to deny a visa to anyone who, in the consul's judgment, would "endanger the public safety of the United States."[3]

During the war years, administrative devices were used to bar refugees, yet they could just as easily have been used to admit refugees. If those in power had wanted to liberalize immigration policy and permit refugee entrance, they could have done so without violating existing law. Roosevelt had made modest changes in policy when he softened the "likely to become a public charge" clause and ordered the extension of German visitors' visas. A more humane refugee policy could have been effected without breaking or changing the Immigration Act, simply through more liberal interpretation. The Treaty-Merchant provision, which permitted entrance to businessmen who showed promise of generating employment, was one option. Temporary immigrants might have been settled in the Virgin Islands. Greater use might have been made of visas for visitors, clergymen, and professors. Children could have been exempted from the quota. Unused portions of quotas could have been redistributed. And "temporary havens" or "free ports" could have been created. (The United States did create a free port, Fort Ontario in Oswego, New York, but it took in fewer than one thousand people.)

The failure to distinguish between an immigrant and a refugee, and the attempt to bar those who were refugees from the United States, was not a policy failure—policymakers reflected the national ethos; it was a moral failure. It remained for President Harry S. Truman to try to reverse established policy and push for a policy of refugee admission. The Truman presidency ushered in the third period of American refugee policy—the era of conscience. Henceforth refugees would be admitted to the United States.

With the surrender of Hitler's military, Truman was faced with an old phenomenon under a name new to the lexicon of human misery—displaced persons. The term "displaced persons" denoted the survivors of the Holocaust and others uprooted by the war who had been expelled or had fled from their homelands and could not return. Responding to their misery, Truman issued a presidential directive that eased their immigration under existing quotas. (The Fort Ontario internees were the immediate beneficiaries of the directive.) But the presidential directive brought in only a trickle of DPs. Dissatisfied with the program, Truman asked Congress to admit DPs outside the quota system. The state was now set for the first postwar policy debate on refugee admissions.

The plight of the DPs had afflicted the consciences of some Americans, effecting a change in the political climate. A newly created pressure group, the Citizens Committee on Displaced Persons (CCDP), led the admissionist forces. The CCDP persuaded Congressman William G. Stratton to introduce a bill to allow one hundred thousand DPs to enter the United States each year for four years. The administration supported the bill and sent Secretary of State George C. Marshall, Secretary of War Robert H. Patterson, and Attorney General Tom C. Clark to Capitol Hill to urge that the bill be passed for foreign-policy reasons. As expected, the bill drew endorsements from religious leaders, but, unexpectedly, the American Federation of Labor reversed its traditional restrictionist position and supported the bill. With pressure mounting, the Senate Judiciary Immigration Subcommittee, under William Chapman Revercomb, a staunch restrictionist, reported out a bill. The DP bill that was eventually enacted outwitted the admissionists.[4]

Under the Displaced Persons Act of 1948, to be eligible for admission to the United States, a DP had to have been in Germany before 22 December 1945. This rendered ineligible the Jewish survivors of concentration camps who had fled to the West after the Polish pogroms of 1946. The bill also gave priority for admission to Balts and those involved in agriculture, thus limiting the numbers available to Jews. The act repealed the Truman directive, and, in order to ensure that existing immigration laws would not be modified, it proposed to admit one hundred thousand DPs under mortgaged quotas. Under the quota system, if all visas for the current year were exhausted, half of the visas for subsequent years could be "mortgaged." Therefore, if displaced persons were admitted from a country, their numbers would not be available for other immigrants from the same countries. (The results of the act proved to be ludicrous. By 1951 the Latvian quota had been mortgaged to the year 2255, the Estonian to 2130, and the Lithuanian to 2079.) President Truman signed the bill reluctantly and a new chapter in refugee policy had begun.

Despite its restrictionist flaws, the Displaced Persons Act was the first significant refugee legislation in American history. In mortgaging future quotas, Congress had recognized that refugee numbers might not be contained within normal immigration quotas. Moreover, in response to humanitarian pressures to admit refugees, the act relaxed earlier restrictive and exclusionary legislation. The act was amended in 1950 and extended in 1951, allowing more than four hundred thousand refugees to find homes in the United States. Although restrictionists had imprinted their bias on the act itself, it is the bureaucracy that makes policy, and the Displaced Persons Commission administered the act liberally.

Refugee admissions had become an important tool in America's Cold War, anticommunist foreign policy. The first major postwar stream of refugees was European escapees from communism, and the Truman and Eisenhower administrations encouraged their flow into the United States. Both the executive and the Congress were committed to encouraging escape from communism, even to the extent of abandoning numerical limits and quotas and allocating funds for escapee assistance. The President's Escapee Program, begun in 1952, was followed in 1953 by the

Refugee Relief Act (RRA) of 1953. The RRA relaxed immigration law by authorizing the issuance of more than two hundred thousand nonquota visas for persons escaping from Iron Curtain countries.

Anticommunist fervor also led to the first mass parole of refugees into the United States. In 1956, just prior to the expiration of the RRA, an anticommunist revolt was crushed in Hungary, and thousands of Hungarian "freedom fighters" fled to Austria. Some were given visas available under the RRA; others, however, at President Eisenhower's direction, were admitted under the obscure attorney general's parole provision of the Immigration and Nationality Act. This was an innovative policy decision—a new and elastic interpretation of parole—but it was in contravention of congressional intent that parole be granted individually, on a case-by-case basis, and that the parolee be required to depart when the purpose of his or her visit had been satisfied.

The Refugee-Escapee Act (REA) of 1957, which admitted still more Hungarians, was significant in two respects. First, in a shift in the immigration law, the act repealed the existing mortgages against the quotas. Second, the REA defined refugee-escapees as victims of racial, religious, or political persecution fleeing Communist or Communist-occupied or -dominated countries, or a country in the Middle East. This definition would stand until the Refugee Act of 1980 amended it. The United States' anticommunist posture led to various policy devices that, beginning in 1959, gave welcome to Cubans fleeing from Castro's revolution.

Other legislation passed in this period of conscience further acknowledged that refugees were distinct from immigrants. In 1960 the passage of the Refugee Fair Share Law responded to the United Nations Declaration of a World Refugee Year. More comprehensive than previous refugee admission programs, the Fair Share Law was designed not to assist refugees of a particular nationality or to meet a particular emergency, but to provide an ongoing mechanism for the admission of refugees for a limited time. Congress authorized the attorney general to use his parole authority to admit twenty-five percent of the total number of refugees from Europe and the Middle East who were not yet permanently resettled. In 1965 the refugee parole program of the Refugee Fair Share Law was terminated and a permanent provision for the admission of refugees was incorporated into basic immigration law. Thus, in piecemeal fashion, refugee admission policy was being developed.

The Migration and Refugee Assistance Act (MRAA) had also been passed in 1962. The policy rationale behind the act was a combination of humanitarianism and realpolitik. The MRAA, the first comprehensive refugee assistance statute, supported programs of assistance to refugees and escapees. It provided for annual contributions to the United Nations High Commissioner for Refugees and the Intergovernmental Committee for European Migration (now the International Organization for Migration) and authorized assistance to refugees overseas and to Cuban refugees in the United States.

The Immigration Act of 1965, which liberalized immigration policy, also specifically addressed the problem of refugees, for the first time providing for their annual admission. Refugees, however, were placed seventh—last—in the preference system for admission to the United States and were allowed the smallest proportion (only six percent, or 10,200 admissions) of all entrants. Family reunification and needed occupational skills took precedence over refugee admissions. The refugee policy that Congress wrote into law also imposed geographic and ideological restrictions. A refugee continued to be defined as an individual fleeing racial, religious, or political persecution from any Communist, Communist-dominated, or Middle Eastern country. Congress also specifically rejected the use of the parole provision for mass admissions.

Congress's first attempt to legislate and regularize refugee admissions, however, was to become obsolete even as it was being constructed. Within the decade, refugees—first Cubans, then Soviet émigrés, and finally Indochinese—would enter the United States in circumvention of statutory policy. Foreign-policy considerations and domestic political pressures would take precedence over statute. American policy toward Cuban refugees was based on anti-Castro communism and nurtured by domestic pressure groups; American policy toward Soviet refugees similarly was predicated on anti-Soviet communism and nurtured by domestic pressure groups. The number of Soviet refugees was significantly smaller than the number of Cubans, whose influx was ongoing, or of Indochinese, who began to arrive in 1975.

In the United States, Jewish pressure groups kept Russian anti-Semitism and discriminatory practices against Jews and other dissidents in the forefront of public opinion. In this, the Jewish pressure groups were substantially aided by a wide spectrum of anticommunist labor, ethnic, and religious groups. In Congress the major attempt to influence Soviet emigration policy was the Jackson-Vanik Amendment to the Trade Reform Act of 1974. Initiated during the Nixon administration, Jackson-Vanik has been a strong influence on American refugee policy toward the Soviets through to the Bush administration. The Nixon administration, in its policy of détente with the Soviets, had, in 1972, worked out a comprehensive commercial agreement with the Soviet government. As part of the agreement, the United States would extend most-favored-nation (MFN) import-tariff treatment to the Soviets. But Henry Jackson in the Senate and Charles Vanik in the House of Representatives introduced an amendment to the East-West trade bill that would have blocked the extension of MFN status and credits to those countries that restricted or taxed the emigration of their citizens. Jackson-Vanik, it was thought, would pressure the Soviet Union to permit freer emigration.

The Jackson-Vanik Amendment, however, seemed to produce the opposite of the desired effect. In the years immediately following the non-implementation of the trade agreement, the Soviets restricted emigration drastically. During the Carter administration, the Soviets wanted a favorable resolution of the Strategic Arms Limitation Treaty and permitted more emigration. But from the Soviet invasion of Afghanistan through the first Reagan administration, emigration continued to plummet, rising again during the second Reagan administration and the Bush presidency. Emigration from the Soviet Union is tied to the general state of American-Soviet relations and is dominated more by Soviet needs than by American refugee policy.

Like the Soviet émigrés, who were, and remain, pawns of superpower politics, the Indochinese were also victims of global rivalries. In the spring of 1975 the Saigon government disintegrated, and in April the United States began evacuating Americans and Vietnamese from Vietnam. The evacuees were admitted into the United States under the parole provisions of the Indochina Refugee Act. Congress responded to the new refugee emergency with the passage of the Migration and Refugee Assistance Act of 1975. The act provided statutory authorization for a temporary program of relief and resettlement. As originally envisioned, the program was to last no later than 1977, but the numbers of Indochinese refugees grew. The world now witnessed the phenomenon of the "boat people." President Jimmy Carter in July 1978 ordered American ships to pick up Indochinese boat people and promised the refugees resettlement in the United States.

In response to the influx of Indochinese refugees, various administrative arrangements were made. President Carter created the post of U.S. Coordinator for Refugee Affairs and the Interagency Coordinating Committee to orchestrate the refugee concerns of the various departments. The Department of State, in response to the refugee crisis, established the Office of Refugee Affairs. The Department of Health Education and Welfare (now the Department of Health and Human Services), which had principal domestic responsibility for refugees, created the Office of Refugee Affairs.

Congress's response to the Indochinese refugee crisis did not stop with the passage of the Migration and Refugee Assistance Act. Representative Joshua Eilberg, chairman of the House Subcommitte on Immigration, Citizenship, and International Law of the Committee on the Judiciary, began a series of hearings on the admission of refugees into the United States. Eilberg's opening statement was significant, for it encapsulated congressional-executive differences that had been building for years. Eilberg pointed out that the vast majority of refugees who entered the United States yearly did so at the discretion of the attorney general, rather than under the regular refugee provisions of the Immigration and Nationality Act of 1965. It was clear that "Congress had abdicated its responsibility." While there was some consultation with Congress when the attorney general exercised his parole power, there was "little if any meaningful input by the Congress or by the members of the Judiciary Committee." Some administrative flexibility was required, but it was not "reasonable or proper for the Congress to delegate to the executive branch its constitutional obligation to enact laws establishing the Nation's refugee policy." The attorney general should not be the sole decision-maker, particularly when there were no legislative guidelines or administrative criteria. Eilberg designed a bill to "establish a uniform refugee policy."[5]

The Eilberg bill, both in its initial and subsequent versions, was restrictive. Parole admission would be limited to twenty thousand; no more than five thousand of such admissions would be available for adjustment to permanent resident status. Fair Share provisions and consultations with the House and Senate were required. In addition, if either house disapproved of the admissions, they could be terminated by resolution. The Eilberg bill never passed.

Congress was growing distressed with the response by the executive branch to the refugee situation. After much delay, in March 1979, the Carter administration submitted a bill, which became law a year later. The Refugee Act of 1980, a watershed for refugee policy, initiated the fourth period in the history of American refugee and asylum policy—the era of legal obligation. The Refugee Act was enacted at a time when America was psychologically awash in post–Vietnam War ambivalence— shame at America's ignominious departure from the Indochina peninsula, coupled with feelings of guilt and responsibility for those who escaped from the area's communist regimes. The media brought the Southeast Asian refugee problem into everyone's home. The parallels to the pre– World War II refugee movements of Europe were obvious; they also were a painful reminder that refusal to help was a decree of death.

The Refugee Act was the culmination of a process that had begun three years earlier. During that period, refugees in ever-growing numbers arrived in the United States, forcing Congress to expand its thinking from a narrow focus on the issues of admissions to a more comprehensive approach that also included domestic resettlement.[6]

When the Refugee Act was being drafted, the House Judiciary Committee report emphasized that "the plight of the refugees themselves as opposed to national-origin or political considerations should be paramount in determining which refugees are to be admitted to the United States."[7] The ideological and geographical biases were to be dropped, the domestic definition was to be linked to the international definition, and the humanitarian and nondiscriminatory aspects of the law were to be emphasized. This has not happened in either refugee or asylee admissions.

Paradoxically, for more than a decade since its passage, the major provisions of the Refugee Act, ideologically neutral admissions and a fair asylum policy, have never been implemented. Who is a refugee and who is an asylee, since the passage of the act, have remained in the forefront as the primary issues of American refugee-asylum policy—a policy conditioned by perceived foreign-policy needs and domestic politics dominated by budgets and interest groups. Since the passage of the Refugee Act, the prime beneficiaries of refugee status have been Southeast Asians, Cubans, and persons departing communist governments in Eastern European and the Soviet Union.

Law and policy diverged because, under the Refugee Act, the executive—in actual practice the Coordinator's Office in the Department of State—submits to the Congress a proposal for refugee admissions for the forthcoming fiscal year. This proposal allocates refugee numbers for each region of the world and is supposed to be the basis for cooperative consultation between the executive and the Congress. Along with the proposed numbers, the State Department presents the rationale for admitting certain groups within each region. (The person must be within a group designated of "special humanitarian concern.") The numbers in fact may apply to particular groups rather than to an entire region; for example, Latin American and the Caribbean had 3,500 slots allocated for fiscal year 1990, but because 3,000 places were reserved for Cuban political prisoners and family members, only 500 spaces remained for the rest of Central and South America.[8]

The regional alloction numbers, however, are suggestive rather than firm. They also can be manipulated to achieve a political purpose. For years, when the State Department knew that the Soviets would not permit emigration, in order to embarrass Moscow, the ceiling on refugees from the Soviet Union was deliberately set artificially high. Admission numbers also can be transferred from one geographical region to another.

Once Congress has approved the State Department's formulas for refugees of special humanitarian concern and its geographical allocations, the actual decisions on admission are made by the Immigration and Naturalization Service (INS) in accordance with a State Department priority system. The INS and State Department, however, may not always agree and problems can arise.

In the early 1980s the INS and the State Department were at loggerheads over processing in Southeast Asia. In 1981, INS officers in Southeast Asia began to review each refugee's application to ascertain whether he or she met the definition of a refugee. As a result the INS rejected nearly all of the thirty-one thousand Khmer applicants, as well as a large number of Vietnamese, as being "economic refugees." The White House intervened and new processing guidelines were issued.[9]

Congress may also intervene. Ordinarily Congress's consultations over refugee admission numbers and regional allocations are cosmetic consultations in which the State Department's position is approved without undue scrutiny. Anticommunist positions have always been politically popular, and so long as the numbers to be admitted are not excessively high and costs are kept concomitantly low, refugee policy arouses the interest of only a few constituencies—affected ethnics, human rights champions, and nongovernmental organizations working with refugees and asylees. But large numbers of refugees incur the fear of a floodtide of newcomers, heavy costs for long-term refugee support, or the attention of a powerful domestic interest group, thus galvanizing the legislature into making refugee or asylum policy. Perhaps the most telling example of congressional intervention in refugee policy involves Soviet émigrés.

The Soviet Union, in a reversal of its closed-door policy, in 1987 opened its doors and the number of Armenians and Jews departing Russia began to rise. The State Department moved to accommodate the new flow. In March 1988 the State Department proposed to increase the worldwide refugee admissions ceiling by 15,000, bringing it to 83,500. While a foreign-policy victory had been won, the opening of the Soviet floodgates created problems with the budget and with pressure groups. As the admission slots filled and the numbers rose, the rules of admission changed. In a dramatic shift, the Reagan administration, having won a long-sought victory, reversed historic policy and began rejecting applications for refugee status from Soviet citizens. INS processing practices changed. U.S. approval for those wanting to depart to the USSR was no longer virtually automatic. In the face of pressures to admit emigrating Soviets, and at the same time not wanting to incur additional costs, the administration resurrected the attorney-general's mass parole power. Parole, although violative of the Refugee Act, was politically viable. It short-circuited admission quotas and did not have the liability of costs. (Parolees may enter the country, but they must pay their own way and do not receive refugee benefits. Theoretically, also, parolees are not eligible for citizenship, although Congress in the past has adjusted parolee status and made them eligible.)

When the Reagan administration, in August 1988, decided to stop according presumptive refugee status to all Soviet applicants and began case-by-case adjudications for Soviets, it set off a controversy. Armenian, Jewish, and Evangelical pressure groups went into action. They convinced Congress that their constituencies suffered systemic persecution. Congress responded and in November 1989 passed the Morrison/Lautenberg Law.[10] This law directs the attorney general to allow for certain nationals (Soviet Jews, Evangelical Christians and other potential targets of persecution in the Soviet Union, and certain nationals of Vietnam, Laos, and Cambodia) a relaxed standard under which to prove a "well-founded fear of persecution." The Morrison/Lautenberg Law is scheduled to expire on 1 October 1992.

While Congress has often concerned itself with refugee admissions, it has paid far less attention to asylum. This was true even when the Refugee Act of 1980 was first being framed. Congress had entirely overlooked the question of asylum, and it was only at the suggestion of the United Nations High Commissioner for Refugees that asylum was provided for in the act. Those provisions, however, were not fully developed, and the discretion to grant asylum was given to the attorney general. In practice, asylum gave the attorney general much of the discretion to admit he had earlier enjoyed under the power to parole. Asylum was not granted on the basis of individual claims, or according to the U.N. standard for persecution, but to members of groups that either advanced the foreign-policy goals of the administration or represented the interests of an important pressure group.

From June 1983 to September 1990, the overall approval rate for asylum cases that were decided was 23.4 percent. But the approval rate for individual countries showed a different picture. The approval rate for the Soviet Union was 76.7 percent; for El Salvador, 2.6 percent, and for Guatemala, 1.8 percent. In 1990 alone the approval rate for the Soviet Union had climbed to 82.4 percent; the rate for El Salvador was 2.5 percent, while for Guatemala it had dropped to 1.4 percent.[11]

As they had for refugees, pressure groups soon went into action. But their arena could not always be the Congress. For redress of asylum grievances, pressure groups had to turn to the courts. The reason was quite simple. The Refugee Act had given the attorney general full decision-making power over asylum decisions, instructing him only to establish the *procedure* by which asylees could be admitted, and setting an annual ceiling of five thousand asylees who could become permanent residents, the first step to citizenship. Congress might question, but it could not intervene in the asylum process. The proper recourse for those who felt that the asylum procedures were being unjustly administered was to the courts.

During the third period of refugee policy, the decade following the passage of the 1980 Refugee Act, a dialectical pattern developed. The Justice Department, impelled by its fear of opening the gates to a flood of refugees, initiated two major policies toward unwanted asylum-seekers: detention and denial of due process. Refugee advocates, in response, brought suit in the courts against these policies; in most of the cases the court ruled against the government. Following each ruling, the government attempted to reinstate its proscribed practices, leading inevitably to still another class-action suit.

Detention was first used as a deliberate government policy in 1981; its purpose, according to an Immigration Task Force, was to reduce the number of individuals asking for asylum. Detention in itself was not illegal. What was illegal were many of the coercive practices employed against those in detention: housing asylum-seekers in dormitories, together with hardened criminals, or in prisons; locating detention centers hundreds of miles from legal representatives; depriving them of proper medical and recreational facilities; confining them to rooms for the entire day; limiting access to mail and telephones; and denying family visits. In certain areas, children have been detained. In short, many of the conditions under which asylum-seekers are detained violate basic prohibitions in the U.N. Convention and Protocol on the Status of Refugees.[12]

Of all the government's policies intended to discourage asylum-seekers, most invidious was its denial of due process. Repeatedly, the Immigration Service has engaged in actions intended to coerce illegal entrants into agreeing to return home or to deny them access to legal representation. In one infamous instance, the INS instituted a program to accelerate asylum hearings for Haitian applicants so as to remove them from the country as quickly as possible. Judges were forced to hear one hundred or more cases in a day; airport inspectors were conducting interviews; it was even recommended that mass hearings be held. For their part, attorneys were subjected to harassment and intimidation; their clients were removed from the state, or even the country, without the attorneys' knowledge.

The program to deport Haitian asylum-seekers led to the first of many successful class-action suits. In the summer of 1980, in *Haitian Refugee Center v. Civiletti,* Judge James Lawrence King ruled that the program, "in its planning and executing, is offensive to every notion of constitutional due process and equal protection."[13] He ordered the government to rehear the Haitians' asylum claims.

Ten years later, in *American Baptist Churches v. Thornburgh,* the court ruled that all Salvadorans and Guatemalans who had been denied asylum since 1980 were entitled to have their cases reopened. As part of the settlement, the INS was required to affirm that "foreign policy and border enforcement considerations, . . . the fact that an individual is from a country whose government the United States supports, . . . [and] whether or not the United States Government agrees with the political or ideological beliefs of the individual [are] not relevant to the determination of whether an applicant for asylum has a well-founded fear of persecution."[14]

The greatest victories of the pressure groups in the area of asylum have been won in the courts, not in the Congress. Ironically, however, when pressure groups did compel the Congress to take action, it was, in effect, to restore a process that the Refugee Act had been intended to curtail— admission by a form of parole. Pressure groups in the United States— most important, the Sanctuary movement—urged the introduction of bills to provide "temporary suspension of deportation for El Salvador refugees." The bill, usually referred to as the DeConcini-Moakley bill, stipulated that Salvadoran nationals who were present in the country on the date the bill was enacted would not be deported for up to three years. A measure on behalf of the Guatemalans asked the attorney general to grant them extended voluntary departure status. Although introduced repeatedly, neither the DeConcini-Moakley bill nor the request for EVD was successful.

Finally, in 1990, as Congress completed work on a broad new immigration law, advocates for the Salvadorans were able to negotiate the inclusion of a safe-haven provision, officially called Temporary Protected Status (TPS). Under the terms of TPS, all Salvadorans in the United States would have an eighteen-month period during which they would not be deported to El Salvador and would be allowed work permits. Should conditions in El Salvador remain dangerous after the eighteen months of TPS expires, the attorney general could extend the status.

The 1980s had been a decade of battles in the courts as well as in the Congress. On the one side was the Justice Department, which, with the support of the executive, did everything in its power to deter and deport unwanted asylum-seekers and those in search of temporary safe haven; on the other side were the supporters of the excluded, who fought for their right to fairness and equity. Now, with the legislation of Temporary Protected Status and the acquiescence of the Immigration Service in the American Baptist Church decision, it appeared that the terms of a truce were being written. In the words of Paul Virtue, Acting General Counsel for the INS, the service now had "little will to do battle."[15]

As the new decade began, the INS was putting into place final asylum regulations, regulations ten years in the making, that are intended to make the asylum process fairer and more consistent. The adjudication process will be removed from the enforcement division of the INS and placed in an independent agency, where adjudicators will be given special training. Rather than using the State Department's Country Reports as the sole source of documentary evidence, the asylum officers will have a wide range of documentation at their disposal. Foreign-policy concerns will no longer be a major influence on asylum decisions, which instead will draw on human rights conditions in the asylum-seeker's country of origin. Whether, in the end, the new procedures will achieve the long-sought justice and equity remains to be seen. It is to be hoped, however, that in this new decade, the energies and resources that were squandered in battle may now be directed toward achieving the intentions of the Refugee Act.

The fifth, or current, period of American refugee and asylum policy is an era of redefinition. For more than a decade since the passage of the Refugee Act, the original intent of Congress to establish a fair, disinterested, and humane refugee-asylum policy was thwarted by the executive; only the federal judiciary acted with fairness and responsibility. The State Department made refugee policy subordinate to its foreign-policy objectives of anticommunism. The Immigration and Naturalization Service gave border control precedence over an enlightened asylum policy. Congress, except when confronted with a specific crisis or spurred to action by powerful pressure groups, took a hands-off attitude toward refugee and asylum policy. But refugee and asylum policies are not made in a vacuum; they have been outpaced by global events.

In May 1991 the Supreme Soviet passed the Law on Entry and Exit; although not due to go into full effect until 1 January 1993, the law nonetheless stands as a milestone victory in the State Department's campaign for free emigration. And in the meantime, Soviet emigration proceeds at an unheard-of pace. (In June 1986 some 2,000 Soviets emigrated; in 1990 more than 370,000 emigrated.)[16] The State Department is now being forced to reassess and redefine its long-held positions.

In Congress, Jackson-Vanik is also being reassessed. Those pressure groups that were instrumental in having Jackson-Vanik passed no longer insist on its retention and are willing to drop it as a reward for Moscow's liberalized emigration policy.

Outside the USSR, the Eastern bloc countries are dismantling Communism and moving toward capitalism and competitive political party systems. East and West Germany have been reunited. Even Albania has cracked. All these momentous changes require a new foreign policy in which fostering emigration is not a cardinal point.

Change, too, is occurring in other parts of the world. A UNHCR-sponsored group of representatives of nongovernmental organizations (NGOs) visited Vietnam in the spring of 1991 and determined that "contrary to prevalent understanding in their home countries of the United States, Canada and Australia, conditions in Vietnam are actually favorable for repatriation."[17] The NGO representatives released a statement citing progress toward a free and open Vietnamese society with rises in personal freedom and private entrepreneurship. With the healing of some of the domestic wounds caused by the Vietnam War, it is now time to try to heal the wounds in Vietnam, Cambodia, and Laos. Healing those wounds requires new directions in Southeast Asian foreign policy.

Closer to home, in Central America, change also is occurring, though less dramatically. The East-West proxy war in Nicaragua has concluded, but continuing unrest in El Salvador and Guatemala has forced large numbers to flee. By granting temporary protected status for Salvadorans in the Immigration Act of 1990, Congress at least has recognized the realities of the region, perhaps a first step in forcing the State Department to redefine its regional foreign policy.

Global political changes have created challenges and opportunities for the executive and the legislature. Both the President and Congress are moving hesitantly and reactively but recognize that new realities call for new policies. It can only be hoped that as new policies emerge, they include a redefined refugee and asylum policy.

Notes

1. For a fuller discussion of the historical periods, see Norman L. Zucker and Naomi Flink Zucker, *The Guarded Gate: The Reality of American Refugee Policy* (New York, 1987), passim.

2. David S. Wyman, *Paper Walls: America and the Refugee Crisis, 1938–1941* (Amherst, Mass., 1968). See also David S. Wyman, *The Abandonment of the Jews: America and the Holocaust, 1941–1945* (New York, 1984).

3. Henry L. Feingold. *The Politics of Rescue: The Roosevelt Administration and the Holocaust, 1938–1945* (New Brunswick, N.J., 1970), 149.

4. For a definitive study of the DP legislation, see Leonard Dinnerstein, *America and the Survivors of the Holocaust* (New York, 1982).

5. U.S. Congress, House of Representatives, Committee on the Judiciary, Hearings Before the Subcommittee on Immigration, Citizenship, and International Law, *Admission of Refugees into the United States*, 95th Cong., 1st sess. (Washington, D.C., 1977), 22.

6. The Refugee Act dealt with four broad areas: (1) the refugee definition and admissions, (2) bureaucratic structure, (3) domestic resettlement, and (4) asylum. The importance of the refugee problem was now bureaucratically recognized in that the Office of the U.S. Coordinator for Refugee Affairs, originally created by executive order, now was statutorily established and the Coordinator was given broad responsibilities for refugee admission and resettlement policy. The act also established an Office of Refugee Resettlement (ORR) within the Department of Health and Human Services and mandated mechanisms for the states to participate in resettlement. The ORR was given a wide range of powers and a variety of federal benefits were given to eligible refugees.

7. U. S. Congress, House of Representatives, *The Refugee Act of 1979*, Report No. 96-608, 96th Cong., 1st sess. (Washington, D.C.: U. S. Government Printing Office, 1979), 13.

8. U.S. Department of State, Coordinator for Refugee Affairs, *Proposed Refugee Admissions for FY 1990* (Washington, D.C., 1989), 13–14.

9. Zucker and Zucker, *The Guarded Gate*, 81–82.

10. For a fuller discussion of the Reagan administration's treatment of Soviet émigrés, see Norman L. Zucker and Naomi Flink Zucker, "The Uneasy Troika in U.S. Refugee Policy: Foreign Policy, Pressure Groups, and Resettlement Costs," *Journal of Refugee Studies* 2:3 (1989): 359–72.

11. Source of statistics: Immigration and Naturalization Service, U.S. Department of Justice, in *Refugee Reports* 11:12 (21 December 1990): 12.

12. Arthur C. Helton, "The Detention of Asylum Seekers in the United States and Canada," paper presented at York University's Centre for Refugee Studies Conference on Refugee Policy: A Comparison of Canada and the U.S.A. (29 May 1990), 15.

13. Zucker and Zucker, *The Guarded Gate*, 198.

14. *Refugee Reports* 11:12 (21 December 1990): 1.

15. *Refugee Reports* 12:1 (29 January 1991): 3.

16. Thomas L. Friedman, "Bush Clears Soviet Trade Benefits and Weighs Role in London Talks," *New York Times*, 4 June 1991.

17. "NGOs Support Progress for the Comprehensive Plan of Action Following UNHCR-Sponsored Visit to Viet Nam," *Monday* 10:12 (10 June 1991): 1–2.

JAMES C. HATHAWAY

The Conundrum of Refugee Protection in Canada: From Control to Compliance to Collective Deterrence

Canadian policy on the protection of refugees has evolved through three distinct traditions. During the first era, refugee protection was constructed as a matter of *immigration control*. Indeed, until the middle of the twentieth century, Canada had no law or policy specifically oriented to the admission of refugees. Refugees simply applied for permission to enter Canada under the auspices of the general immigration scheme, the primary purpose of which was to promote domestic economic interests. The erosion of this historical view of refugees as immigrants has occurred only gradually, such that even today most refugees protected by Canada must meet immigration selection criteria, in addition to showing that they are at risk in their home country.

Since the mid-1960s, however, Canada has been engaged in the process of balancing and constraining this immigration-based view of refugee protection in consequence of its undertaking to *comply with international legal obligations* owed to refugees. During this second era, domestic determination schemes and expanded overseas resettlement efforts have been established as means of admitting internationally identified refugees to permanent residency in Canada. During the 1990s, Canada is poised to become primarily a country of first asylum, with almost half of its refugee intake no longer subject to immigration control.

The probable third era of refugee protection will be defined as a reaction to the second. Even as Canada has reluctantly but faithfully moved to implement its duty to protect refugees, European states have commenced a process of *collective deterrence*, intended to minimize protection opportunities in that continent. The result has been a deflection of claimants from Europe to Canada, to the point that only about 20 percent of

JOURNAL OF POLICY HISTORY, Vol. 4, No. 1, 1992.

those who seek asylum in Canada each year originate in the Western Hemisphere. Observers contend that a fair and open determination system cannot withstand the pressures generated by the diminution of asylum opportunities in Europe, and they urge Canada to join the protectionist club. Canada's asylum dilemma in this third era will therefore center on the viability of a continued commitment to multilateral refugee protection as contemplated by the Refugee Convention in the context of an effective renunciation of responsibility by many of its traditional allies.

The Situation-Specific Approach to Refugee Protection

Canada first confronted the refugee phenomenon at the close of World War II.[1] Even though there were millions of European refugees to be protected, Canada responded cautiously by seeking out only the most "adaptable" European refugees from among those in need of resettlement.[2] The Canadian response to the European refugee crisis included the Sponsored Labor Movement, pursuant to which Canada assisted highly skilled workers in the refugee population to immigrate; the Close Relatives Scheme, which allowed Canadians to bring in family members from among the displaced population of Europe; and the admission to Canada of orphaned children under the sponsorship of domestic ethnic and religious groups. All of these refugees were capable of ready assimilation in Canada and could reasonably be expected to make few demands on national resources. In stark contrast, Canada refused to admit any of the "hardcore" European refugee population, including thousands of persons whose age, illness, or handicap made them undesirable immigrants.[3]

Between 1956 and 1972, Canada enacted other situation-specific refugee programs, which resulted in the admission of more than 37,000 Hungarians, nearly 11,000 Czechs, and more than 7,000 Ugandan Asians. These several refugee movements subsequent to World War II marked the beginning of a Canadian refugee policy in that they were demonstrative of an evolving willingness on the part of the government to respond directly to refugee flows. This new approach was carefully confined, however, by a strategic orientation: refugees were seen as the proper beneficiaries of special concern only insofar as their admission was consonant with more general political objectives.[4] Too, all of these programs were of limited duration and scope, and as such did not signal a general openness to refugee resettlement. Most important, none of these refugee movements was inconsistent with the underlying economic determinants of Canadian immigration policy, as the majority of the refugees were educated and skilled and were thus poised to make a positive contribution to Canada's economic prosperity.

The Codification of Canadian Refugee Policy

Canada participated actively in the drafting of the 1951 Convention relating to the Status of Refugees, but it did not sign the accord. The Department of Citizenship and Immigration was of the view that the Convention was inconsistent with Canadian interests both because its definition was conceptually open-ended and because the duty to avoid the return of refugees might inhibit Canada's ability to turn away undesirable immigrants.[5] The general view was that accession would need to be significantly and perhaps unacceptably conditioned in order to tailor Canadian obligations under the Convention to immigration policy:

> We admire the spirit of the Convention and are guided by it; however, to endeavour to accede to the letter of the Convention would only prove confusing and perhaps harmful to its welfare in the light of current Canadian legislation.[6]

The Department was particularly troubled by the general practice of state parties to the Convention to extend protection to refugees from all regions of the world, rather than opting into the Convention's geographical limitation clause.[7] It was argued that the prevailing Canadian policy of institutionalized racism would prohibit the assumption of any duties of universal scope:

> . . . refugees, defined in Article IA [of the Refugee Convention] could include some Asiatics; in such event the provisions of P.C. 2115 would be applicable and they may be deemed to conflict with the [nondiscrimination] provisions of [the Refugee Convention].[8]

Senior immigration officials of the 1950s favored retention of a bureaucratically formulated refugee definition, which focused on the admission of ideological émigrés from the East Bloc. The operational refugee definition allowed discretion to be exercised to facilitate the entry of any person who

> (a) as a result of events arising out of World War II, [was] displaced from one European country to another, e.g. from an Eastern to a

Western European country, and [had] not been permanently resettled; or

(b) because of fear or dissatisfaction[9] [had] left [one of twelve Eastern
European countries] since closure of the International Refugee Organization . . . and [had] not been permanently re-settled.[10]

This conceptual approach, however, was opposed by the Department of
External Affairs, which was concerned to advance Canada's role as a
major player in the field of international human rights law. Since at least
1954, External Affairs appealed to the Department of Citizenship and
Immigration to agree to accede to the Refugee Convention as a means of
securing gains within "the broad context of Canadian international relations."[11] The External Affairs Department attempted to explain away the
concerns of immigration officials in regard to the open-ended scope of the
Convention by arguing that "the Canadian Government would in any
case always have the right to decide whether or not to accept the refugees,
no matter how 'open-ended' the Convention might be interpreted."[12]
Moreover, External Affairs confidently asserted that immigration officials
could turn away any undesirable refugees at the port of entry since "the
Conference which drafted the Convention considered this point and
rejected any suggestion that [the duty of non-refoulement] applied to the
admission of refugees."[13] The Deputy Minister of Citizenship and Immigration, George Davidson, disagreed. On the advice of UNHCR, he argued
that the practice of the international community was to apply the Convention refugee definition in a largely open-ended way, and to respect the
norm of nonreturn in regard to refugees at a port of entry on the same
footing as those already physically present in Canada. While Canada
might refuse to adopt customary practice, the Deputy Minister saw "little
to be gained in signing the Refugee Convention and then trying to maintain an interpretation of the important definition of 'refugee' that is
clearly contrary to the interpretation unanimously placed on it by the
present signatories."[14] He concluded in 1961 that "about all that we can
do now is let the matter drop."[15]

The issue of accession to the Refugee Convention was revived after the
election of the Pearson government in 1963. Lester Pearson, a leading
architect of the United Nations and former president of its General Assembly, was anxious that Canada play a major role in the promotion of
multilateralism through the United Nations system.[16] In this atmosphere,
the new Deputy Minister of Immigration, C. M. Isbister, proposed the
reconsideration of adopting the Convention into Canadian law.[17] The
Immigration Branch had by this point determined that Canada's treat-

ment of refugees was as generous as that provided by any state that had signed the Refugee Convention; that the Convention provided a helpful structure upon which to establish a domestic refugee determination authority; and, that from the perspective of international public relations, Canada was "already carrying all the burdens of responsibility in refugee matters, but [its] highly legalistic refusal to accede to the 1951 Convention has prevented [Canada] from getting much of the credit [it] should have."[18] Moreover, immigration authorities suggested that Canada should apply the Convention definition to refugees from around the world rather than just protecting European refugees.[19]

This fundamental shift in policy was carried forward in the government's 1966 White Paper on Immigration,[20] resulting in Canada's accession to the Convention and Protocol in 1969. The cold-war-derived Canadian definition of refugee status that had governed domestic immigration practice since the postwar years was now clearly anomalous:

> Our present definition lacks detail as to the causes of fear. It omits any reference to race, religion, nationality, membership of a particular social group or political opinion as a ground for persecution. The definition thus appears to be exclusively politically orientated, an orientation also reflected in the restrictions imposed by listing European countries deemed to be Canada's adversaries in the cold war with the Communist world. The definition is very restricted in time. It omits, too, important reasons for the loss of or ineligibility for refugee status such as are found in the Convention. It is orientated towards Europe at a time when we boast of a global view . . .[21]

As a result, the Immigration Appeal Board Act was amended in 1973 to provide the first Convention-based standard for refugee admissions to Canada.[22] The amendments, which applied only to refugee claims made from within Canada, permitted the Immigration Appeal Board to quash a deportation order whenever it determined that there were "reasonable grounds for believing that the person concerned [was] a refugee protected by the [United Nations] Convention."[23]

The procedure established by this enactment proved to be an inadequate means of implementing Canada's obligations under the Refugee Convention for two reasons. First, it was wholly within the Board's discretion to grant or withhold landing in any particular case.[24] As such, there was no guarantee that refugees would in fact receive protection from Canada. Second, because the refugee claim could be raised only on appeal rather than at the immigration inquiry itself, those persons whose cases did not proceed beyond the initial hearing had no means of vindicating their claims to refugee status.[25]

The Establishment of an Asylum Process in Canada

The next major step in the evolution of refugee protection in Canada was the preparation of a parliamentary green paper on immigration policy in 1975,[26] which led to the drafting of the 1976 Immigration Act.[27] Two aspects of the new legislation were of critical importance in determining the scope of refugee protection in Canada. First, the Convention refugee definition was formally incorporated in Canadian law and a process established to adjudicate all claims to asylum. Second, as will be discussed in the next section, Canada's discretionary refugee admissions efforts were extended to a broader class of internationally unprotected persons.

Notwithstanding the clear political commitment to the adoption of a Convention-based regime, there was persistent bureaucratic opposition to the establishment of a formal process for the inland adjudication of claims to refugee status based on the international definition. On the one hand, the argument was made on the basis of a possible "magnet effect," which would erode the effectiveness of overseas screening processes:

> A policy of first asylum, established in law and universally proclaimed, would serve primarily to attract to our ports of entry each year many hundreds, probably thousands, of refugees and others seeking not temporary refuge but resettlement, persons whose applications could and should have been processed by our posts abroad.[28]

Even those within the government who understood the importance of implementation of international obligations were disinclined to do more than establish the minimum level of protection:

> We have an excellent record in accepting refugees, oppressed minorities and vicitms of natural disaster, but do we want to be *forced* to do so? I submit that aside from the carefully defined responsibilities in the UN Convention and Protocol, our acceptance of these people should be a matter of discretion.[29]

This protectionist stance led the government to draft legislation based on the principle that Canada would accept "neither more nor less than its obligations under the Convention."[30] The "exact wording of the [United

Nations] definition of refugee"[31] would be incorporated in the new immigration law,[32] and Canada would stop short of granting refugees any right to enter or remain in its territory.

> For obvious reasons . . . it is necessary to preclude any suggestion in the language of the Act that displacement or persecution in itself confers an entitlement to enter Canada on the persons affected.[33]

Thus, section 3(g) of the new Immigration Act recited as an objective of Canadian immigration policy the need "to fulfil Canada's international legal obligations with respect to refugees, and to uphold its humanitarian tradition with respect to the displaced and persecuted."[34] Persons in Canada who met the Convention definition as codified in the Act were to be protected from removal to a country in which persecution was feared,[35] but the decision to grant or withhold permanent resident status remained, at least in theory, an immigration prerogative.

Expanded Refugee Protection in a Discretionary Context

At present, then, the only persons with an entitlement to protection in Canada are those who meet the definition of refugee status derived from the Convention and Protocol. None of the more expansive variants of the refugee concept recognized in international law has been adopted for the purpose of recognizing a *right* to asylum in Canada.[36] Nonetheless, broadened conceptions of refugee status have influenced discretionary admission and resettlement policies. This approach is in line with the recommendation in 1975 of a senior immigration official that Canadian law should

> define "refugee" strictly and concisely. . . . Other deserving groups might then be slotted into a string of supplementary, "non-refuge" categories [which] . . . we would then regard . . . as ordinary immigrants, subject to deportation, etc. In short, we should draw a clear legal distinction between a relatively narrow category of "refugees" and a much wider (and changing) assortment of threatened classes deserving of special attention although not the full range of post-arrival benefits conferred upon "refugees."[37]

Canada has made a significant contribution to the resettlement of both Convention refugees outside Canadian jurisdiction and of persons in refugee-like situations outside the scope of the Convention. The expanded scope of protection for involuntary migrants stemmed from the decision by Canadian immigration officials in 1969 to commence the resettlement of refugees from developing countries as part of a more universal, nondiscriminatory refugee policy.[38] This policy commitment has been carried out in two ways. First, Canadian consular authorities are authorized to process the applications for admission of persons who are Convention refugees but who have no claim in law to Canadian protection because they remain abroad.[39] Second, Canadian legislation provides for the overseas selection of displaced and persecuted persons who require resettlement and assistance on humanitarian grounds.[40] This mandate is implemented through the designation of refugee-like classes, which currently include certain nationals of Chile, El Salvador, and Guatemala (the Political Prisoners and Oppressed Persons Designated Class);[41] of Kampuchea (the Indochinese Designated Class);[42] and of Laos and Vietnam (the Indochinese Designated Class, Transitional).[43] Until 1990, the government also maintained a Self-Exiled Persons Designated Class,[44] which facilitated the admission of the nationals of Eastern European states.

The apparent liberality of these expansions of the Canadian refugee concept, however, masks an underlying intention to avoid the uncertainties inherent in a policy of first asylum by contributing to refugee relief in a way that permits the interposition of domestic economic and social priorities. Because persons *outside* the scope of Canada's obligations under the Convention (because they are not within Canadian territory, they do not meet the Convention refugee definition, or both) are not in a position to assert any duty on the part of Canada to admit them, Canada can *select* non-Convention refugees on the basis of its general immigration policies. Refugees who are unable to invoke rights under the Convention can "be dealt with in the same manner as other immigrants, but [are] coded as refugees for statistical purposes."[45] Thus, it is not enough that applicants meet the Convention definition of a refugee or fall within the scope of one of the refugee-like "designated classes."[46] Eligibility is rather restricted, first, to persons who have not been permanently resettled elsewhere.[47] Applicants who have not been authorized to work in their country of first asylum or who have no long-term right of residence are the intended beneficiaries of the program. Second, it must be ascertained that the refugee is not inadmissible to Canada[48] because, for example, he or she has a criminal record[49] or is likely to make excessive demands on Canadian health or social services.[50] Finally, and perhaps most important, the refugee must be deemed capable of "successful establishment in

Canada."[51] In making this determination, the availability to the refugee of financial or other assistance (such as may be provided by a sponsoring group or organization), as well as such traditional immigration criteria as personal motivation, education, experience, and the demand in Canada for persons with comparable skills are considered.[52] This enhanced ability to *control* the admission of non-Convention refugees has contributed to making overseas resettlement a more administratively palatable focus for Canadian refugee protection efforts.[53]

During the period 1991–95, the government plans to resettle 13,000 refugees per annum (including Convention refugees and members of designated classes).[54] It is expected that 35 percent will come from Southeast Asia, 25 percent from Latin America, 22 percent from the Middle East and West Africa, 13 percent from Africa, and 5 percent from Eastern Europe.[55] Direct government resettlement quotas are supplemented by an open-ended private sponsorship program,[56] under which private groups and nongovernmental organizations agree to bear the cost of resettlement assistance.[57] Private sponsorship is predicted to result in the resettlement of an average of 18,700 refugees per year during 1991–95.[58] Taken together, government and private resettlement efforts will account for approximately 60 percent of total refugee admissions, the balance (an average of 22,000 per annum) being made up of persons admitted under the inland determination system.[59]

Canada's Emergence as a Country of First Asylum

During the first half of the 1990s, Canada will come close to being predominantly a country of first asylum, with the overseas resettlement process declining quite dramatically in relative importance within the overall Canadian refugee protection program. By 1995, it is estimated that the inland determination system will account for as many refugee landings as will combined government and private resettlement efforts.[60] This is a significant shift from the 1980s, when only about one-quarter of refugee landings resulted from domestic administrative and quasi-judicial determination programs.[61]

Any account of the Canadian inland determination system must first recognize that the number of claimants entering the Canadian system has been artificially constrained by the persistence of immigration authorities in maintaining visa requirements for the nationals of many refugee-producing states:[62]

Canada is buffered from large scale [refugee] flows by the United States and, to a lesser extent, by Europe. What the government does to reinforce or counteract those buffers affects how accessible Canada is to people who do not submit to selection abroad, or who are in such circumstances that they cannot do so. The record of successive governments in imposing visa requirements on sources of refugee claims emphasizes the policy choice.[63]

Because a visa will not be issued for the purpose of making a refugee claim in Canada,[64] only those who either lie about their intentions or secure forged documentation are able successfully to satisfy the queries of the transportation company employees who administer Canadian law abroad.[65] Most refugees in these states, however, are simply barred from accessing the Canadian determination system.

Until the recent refugee law reform, Canada administered two distinct inland refugee protection systems for those who managed to outmaneuver overseas deterrence efforts. Most of Canada's refugee admissions were made on the basis of an administrative process styled the "special measures program," which was a means of protecting persons arriving in Canada from countries that were experiencing war or domestic turmoil.[66] The second initiative was a more formal process intended to identify Convention refugees, administered in the first instance by the Refugee Status Advisory Committee, with the possibility of an appeal to the Immigration Appeal Board.

The special measures program authorized the issuance of a stay of execution on removal orders against persons from such countries as Chile, El Salvador, Guatemala, Iran, Lebanon, and Sri Lanka who were physically present in Canada.[67] Nationals of these countries were generally issued with limited-duration employment authorizations, upon the expiration of which they were interviewed by immigration authorities. Insofar as the applicant met the test for successful establishment in Canada (he or she was working, spoke or was learning an official language, and showed realistic plans for future self-support), a grant of landing on the basis of relaxed criteria could be made.[68] In addition, most of the programs provided for the expedited sponsorship of family members from the countries concerned.[69]

In February 1987, however, the inland protection aspect of these initiatives was summarily canceled as part of the government's refugee law reform. Citing concern over the potential for abuse by persons not genuinely in need of protection, the government announced that the programs would be "modified to focus [exclusively] on overseas processing . . . of the relatives of Canadians affected by events in these countries."[70] The ending of the inland special measures program represented a major conceptual shift toward restrictionism in Canadian refugee protection efforts, as the scope of this program most closely approximated the use of a broadened refugee definition as the basis for according a *right* to protection: it offered the only means whereby a non-Convention refugee could receive temporary asylum in Canada without the necessity of satisfying discretionary admissions criteria. The demise of special measures initiatives signaled Canada's determination to limit efforts on behalf of the expanded class of refugees to programs that have a substantial immigration-based criterion, and to allow only Convention refugees to receive protection on the ground of their need alone.

In contrast to the administrative special measures program, claims to Convention refugee status under the 1976 legislation were decided on the basis of an advisory opinion provided to the Minister by a committee that had reviewed a transcript of the claimant's formal examination under oath. This system was disbanded in consequence of the landmark *Singh* decision of the Supreme Court of Canada,[71] which held that the examination-under-oath process constituted an unwarranted infringement of the right of refugee claimants to an oral hearing. The government's answer was the establishment in 1989 of the quasi-judicial Convention Refugee Determination Division (CRDD) of the Immigration and Refugee Board, which is now the sole authority charged with the protection of refugees in Canada.

The benefits of the new CRDD hearing process were initially overshadowed by the government's unfortunate decision to advance a distinctly protectionist agenda as part of the same legislative reform that established the CRDD.[72] The new legislation gave the Minister of Immigration the power to interdict ships at sea and to turn away vessels with undocumented aliens aboard without determining any claims to refugee status.[73] Refugees who managed to arrive in Canada could be excluded from the hearing process and returned to an intermediate country judged by the federal cabinet to be "safe," notwithstanding any fear of persecution the claimant might have.[74] Persons suspected of assisting undocumented refugees to make claims in Canada could be criminally prosecuted and imprisoned.[75] In fact, however, the power to interdict at sea was allowed to expire without having been exercised; the "safe third-country" exclusion system has not been implemented by cabinet, and there have been no prosecutions of persons involved in refugee protection. In the result, it is mainly the positive aspects of the reform that survive.

Under the new procedure, refugee claimants first appear before an immigration adjudicator and a member of the CRDD to establish their eligibility to proceed to status determination and the credible basis of their claim.[76] This initial hearing stage, administered by Immigration Canada,[77] has been the source of greatest delay in the determination process, with as much as a year elapsing between arrival in Canada and the eligibility decision.[78] Because the "safe third-country" exclusion process has not been declared in force, however, more than 90 percent of claimants do eventually proceed to a full hearing of their claim before a CRDD panel.[79] In recognition of the fact that few abusive claims are in fact being made at present, and in the hope of decreasing systemic delays, immigration authorities have recently instituted the Simplified Inquiry Process (SIP).[80] Instead of requiring a formal first-level hearing, the SIP authorizes the making of a positive decision on eligibility and credible basis *pro forma* upon the recommendation of an immigration official who has reviewed the file and considered the prevailing referral and acceptance record for persons from the claimant's country of origin. In practical terms, therefore, the first-level hearing is being transformed by policy into a means of segregating out unfounded claims, the approach preferred by most of those who opposed the government's decision to establish a universal two-level hearing system.

Claimants referred forward from the first-level hearing are then entitled to a quasi-judicial hearing convened before two members of the CRDD.[81] Only one of the two CRDD members who sit on each case needs to decide in the claimant's favor for recognition to ensue. Claimants have access to government-funded translation and, in some provinces, to legal aid representation. The process is intended to be nonadversarial, in consequence of which it is facilitated by a Refugee Hearing Office who acts as counsel to the CRDD panel, and access is provided to a computerized country data system maintained by the Board's documentation center.

As its chairman recently noted, the CRDD has had to cope with an extraordinary range of logistical challenges.[82] Most significant, the CRDD was initially resourced to handle only half of the 36,000 refugee claims now made in Canada each year; and the real impact of the increased number of claimants is exacerbated by the fact that few persons arriving in Canada have presented claims that are either ineligible or lacking a credible basis, thus radically increasing the number of full hearings required. In response, changes have recently been made to increase efficiency at the full-hearing stage. First, the number of CRDD members and hearing rooms have been significantly increased. At some offices, members are allowed to specialize by geographical region, thereby reducing hearing time as a function of enhanced expertise. Second, and most important, an Expedited Process for claimants from major source countries with a high acceptance rate has restored to inland determination some of the speed and flexibility formerly associated with the special-measures programs.

Under the Expedited Process,[83] a claimant referred from the first-level hearing may be recommended to the CRDD for recognition by a Refugee Hearing Officer who has reviewed the file and conducted an informal interview with the claimant. An agreed statement of facts goes forward to a single CRDD member, who may simply endorse the recommendation, failing which the claim proceeds to a full hearing in the ordinary course before two members of the CRDD. While the eligible countries vary as a function of volume of refugee flow and adjudicative outcome, the nationals of El Salvador, Ethiopia, Iran, Lebanon, Pakistan, Somalia, and Sri Lanka have recently been included within the ambit of the Expedited Process. As citizens of these countries are also likely to have been "waved through" the first-level hearing, the net result is a very significant decrease in the processing time for persons from known refugee-producing states. The combined result of these changes at the second level is that cases are now generally opened and decided within three months after referral from the first-level hearing, with an average of 3,000 second-level hearings taking place each month.[84]

Appeal rights are limited at both levels:[85] an application for judicial review of a first-level hearing may be made to the Federal Court, but it will not ordinarily delay the execution of a removal order. An appeal from the second-level decision of the CRDD requires leave of the Federal Court, although claimants may remain in Canada pending the outcome of that application. Persons ultimately found to be Convention refugees are now granted a qualified right to remain in Canada on a permanent basis.[86]

During its first two years of operation, the CRDD has finally determined the claims of more than 21,000 applicants from over one hundred countries, with an average net positive recognition rate in excess of 70 percent.[87] The major source countries for refugees who claim status in Canada are China, El Salvador, Iran, Lebanon, Somalia, and Sri Lanka, which collectively accounted for nearly 50 percent of refugee arrivals during the first quarter of 1991.[88] There is, however, quite a variation in primary countries of origin among the CRDD's four regions. In British Columbia, Chinese and Iranians are the two largest claimant groups; in the the Prairie Provinces, Salvadorans and Guatemalans dominate; in Ontario, most claimants are from Somalia or Sri Lanka; and in the Quebec and Atlantic region, Bulgaria and Lebanon have been the two most common countries of origin.[89] The high recognition rate in Canada reflects this pattern of arrivals from states known for strife or serious abuse, coupled with the evolution of a jurisprudence committed to the progressive interpretation of the Convention-refugee definition in a human rights context.[90]

The Conundrum of Refugee Protection in Canada

From the perspective of maximizing protection opportunities, three major weaknesses exist in Canada's new determination system. First, immigration officials continue to resort to crude methods of deterrence through the imposition of visa controls on refugee-producing states, resulting in the screening out of many genuine Convention refugees.[91] Second, the "safe third-country" disentitlement principle could be implemented by cabinet at any time. While it is unclear whether or not the United States and Europe would in fact be willing to take back those claimants targeted by the "safe third-country" exclusion,[92] the lower recognition rates in these intermediate states suggests a probable reduction in net protection opportunities if implementation were to occur. Third, and perhaps most ironic, immigration officials have failed to remove from Canada most persons found not to be Convention refugees, thereby creating the risk of a spate of nongenuine claims sufficient to cripple the determination system.[93] It is of particular concern that policy jurisdiction to counteract each of these major threats to the viability of the Canadian determination system lies not with the Immigration and Refugee Board, but rather with the very immigration bureaucracy that has long argued for a de-emphasis on inland asylum efforts in favor of overseas refugee resettlement.[94]

As serious as these defects are, however, they pale in comparison with the impending prospect of Canada joining the systematic efforts of European states to reduce the procedural rights of refugees to the lowest common denominator, and to enforce severe limitations on the ability of refugees to seek out a place of asylum.[95]

For the more than 80 percent of refugee claimants who come to Canada from outside the Western Hemisphere,[96] Canada is not a geographically logical country of asylum. Because distances between Canada and Asia, Africa, and the Middle East are substantial, and because there are few nonstop transportation linkages between Canada and these regions, the motivation of claimants from these areas to seek asylum in Canada must derive from something other than simple convenience. The decision of these refugees to bypass Europe logically stems from a belief that they are more likely to be recognized as refugees in Canada, or that the quality of protection and life in Canada is superior to that afforded refugees in Europe. Whichever hypothesis is accurate, it follows that insofar as European governments constrain access to quality asylum, the Canadian system is likely to see an increase in refugee applications. While the inferior procedural safeguards and recognition rates in most of Europe have no doubt already led many refugees to come to Canada, the implementation of the Schengen[97] and Dublin[98] agreements can be expected to exacerbate significantly this move away from Europe.

This is Canada's asylum dilemma. If Canada continues to administer fairly its inland refugee determination system in the context of a *de facto* renunciation of collective responsibility by the majority of industrialized states, it will undoubtedly be confronted by a dramatic rise in protection requests. Faced with this demand for asylum, Canada will have several choices. First, it might simply rethink its immigration mix in which refugee admissions are limited to about 20–25 percent of Canada's total immigration intake. This is unlikely, however, given the strong domestic support for family reunification and business immigration programs.[99] A second alternative would be for a much more restrictive interpretation to be given to the Convention refugee definition and to the procedural safeguards afforded refugee claimants in Canada. This tack, however, is likely to be stymied by the compelling jurisprudence developed to date and the dictates of Canada's constitutional culture.[100] Third, and most probable as an initial response, immigration officials may strengthen unilateral overseas deterrence efforts, primarily through visa controls. This may prove partly effective but is unlikely to prevent the flow of truly desperate humanity, as experience with the prevailing visa-control policy demonstrates.[101]

Ultimately, Canada likely will follow the protectionist lead of European states. Indeed, a draft report of the Law Reform Commission of Canada has already posited this option, even while candidly admitting that European harmonization schemes are "not free of criticism":[102]

> A central weakness of present "safe third country" provisions . . . lies in their formulation in substantive, rather than procedural terms. It is therefore recommended that Canada associate itself closely with developments in Europe, with a view to reformulating existing "safe third country" provisions on the basis of future treaty arrangements with *like-minded States* party to the 1951 Convention/1967 Protocol [emphasis added].[103]

The problem, of course, is that agreements like the Dublin and Schengen conventions are not intended to establish collective responsibility for protection, but rather to prevent refugees from upsetting political equilibrium within Europe. These accords do not institute community monitoring of clearly defined procedural standards for status determination, much less mandate fair-minded interpretations of the Convention refugee definition. Rather, they simply prevent refugees from making choices about where they will seek asylum, without any concomitant duty on states to eliminate deterrence schemes. Moreover, the harmonization agreements give states an incentive to offer only the lowest common denominator of protection, since to do otherwise will lead them to take responsibility for a disproportionate share of the collective duty.

Canada's accession to this regime would therefore weaken the overall quality of protection available to refugees in the West. Yet logistically and politically, the option of continuing to deal unilaterally with refugees is also unpalatable, since Canada would have difficulty absorbing the refugee flow likely to be diverted from Europe. Canada's conundrum therefore bears witness to the imperative to rethink the nature and structure of the international refugee protection regime, which erroneously assumes the willingness of states to achieve a collective end through voluntary, independent action.[104]

Osgoode Hall Law School, York University

Notes

1. David Dewitt and John Kirton, *Canada as a Principal Power* (Toronto, 1983), 245–46.

2. ". . . The policy that gradually allowed the arrival of displaced persons remained rooted in the traditional criteria of economic absorptive capacity and concern over homogeneity of population characteristics": ibid., at 246.

3. Gerald Dirks, *Canada's Refugee Policy: Indifference or Opportunism?* (Montreal, 1977), 158.

4. "The international context seemed to place Canada, along with its allies, in a position of responsibility to offer assistance to those who suffered at the hands of Communist repression": Dewitt and Kirton, note 1 above, at 251. In the case of the Ugandan Asians, Canada's preparedness to act was in large part a response to the urgent needs of its mother country, the United Kingdom: Guy Goodwin-Gill, *International Law and the Movement of Persons Between States* (Oxford, 1978), 212–13.

5. "One of the major difficulties we have with the Convention is that by interpretation of the High Commissioner's Office and practice of States who have so far become signatories, it can embrace almost anyone from behind the Iron Curtain and other areas who chooses to seek refugee status outside of his own country. It represents an open-ended commitment in this respect. . . . [A]rticle 33 of the Convention which may not be reserved, limits the grounds on which deportation may be ordered and limits the countries to which deportation may be effected. Our Immigration Act contains no such limitations": Memorandum to the Minister of Citizenship and Immigration from C. M. Isbister, Deputy Minister of Citizenship and Immigration, 2 December 1963, File 566-10.

6. Memorandum to the Director of Immigration, Department of Citizenship and Immigration from the Executive Assistant, 6 September 1960, File 566-9. *Accord* Memorandum to the Under-Secretary of State for External Affairs from Laval Fortier, Deputy Minister of Citizenship and Immigration, 8 July 1954, File 566-10.

7. Memorandum to the Minister of Citizenship and Immigration from Laval Fortier, Deputy Minister of Citizenship and Immigration, 29 May 1958, File 566-10.

8. Memorandum to the Deputy Minister of Citizenship and Immigration from the Director of Immigration, 19 January 1953, File 566-10.

9. "In 1966, the definition was altered to exclude the 'economic' refugee by deleting the phrase 'or dissatisfaction.' This revision was made primarily to exclude Yugoslavians who had left their country for such countries as West Germany, Austria and Italy from which they hoped to migrate to other countries including Canada": Memorandum to the Director, Planning Branch, Department of Manpower and Immigration from A. J. Banerd, 23 November 1967, File 5780-1.

10. Memorandum to the Director of Administrative Services from the Director of Immigration, 8 March 1961, File 566-10.

11. Memorandum to George Davidson, Deputy Minister of Citizenship and Immigration from Norman Robertson, Under-Secretary of State for External Affairs, 5 July 1961, File 566-9. *Accord* Memorandum to the Deputy Minister of Citizenship and Immigration from the Acting Under-Secretary of State for External Affairs, 18 February 1954, File 566-10; and Memorandum to Laval Fortier, Deputy Minister of Citizenship and Immigration from Jules Leger, Under-Secretary of State for External Affairs, 11 January 1957, File 566-10.

12. Memorandum to C. M. Isbister, Deputy Minister of Citizenship and Immigration from Norman Robertson, Under-Secretary of State for External Affairs, 18 December 1963, File 566-9.

13. Ibid. It has since been established that the duty of non-refoulement of refugees applies equally within the territory of a state and at its frontiers: Guy Goodwin-Gill, *The Refugee in International Law* (Oxford, 1983), 74–78.

14. Letter to Norman Robertson, Under-Secretary of State for External Affairs, from George Davidson, Deputy Minister of Citizenship and Immigration, 6 October 1961, File 566-9.

15. Ibid.

16. "Support for the United Nations was a major element in Canada's foreign policy. . . . The early breakdown between the Big Powers in the United Nations, on whose co-operation so much of the Charter was based, made the position of the Middle Powers such as Canada more important than it would otherwise have been. . . . [Middle Powers] stood between the increasing number of small states which had little power and the great states which had too much. Canada was one of the most active of these Middle Powers": Lester Pearson, *Mike: The Memoirs of the Rt. Hon. Lester B. Pearson* (Toronto, 1973), vol. 2, 121.

17. Letter to Marcel Cadieux, Under-Secretary of State for External Affairs, from C. M. Isbister, Deputy Minister of Immigration, 1 December 1964, File 566-9.

18. Memorandum to File from J. L. Manion, Immigration Branch, 1 December 1964, File 566-9.

19. Letter to the Under-Secretary of State for External Affairs from R. B. Curry, Assistant Deputy Minister of Immigration, 14 December 1965, File 566-9.

20. Christopher Wydrzynski, "Refugees and the Immigration Act," *McGill Law Journal* 25 (1979): 159.

21. Memorandum to the Director, Planning Branch, Department of Manpower and Immigration, note 9 above, at 8.

22. *Immigration Appeal Board Act*, R.S.C. 1970, c.I-3 ("Immigration Appeal Board Act").

23. *An Act to Amend the Immigration Appeal Board Act*, S.C. 1973–74, c.27, ss.1,5.

Prior to this amendment, "political opinion" was often invoked as a ground for landing under the Immigration Appeal Board's general equitable jurisdiction.

24. Section 15(b)(i) of the Immigration Appeal Board Act as amended (ibid.) permitted, but did not require, the Board to quash a deportation order where it was of the view that the applicant was a refugee protected by the Convention.

25. Pursuant to section 11 of the Immigration Appeal Board Act as amended, note 23 above, claimants were entitled to have their appeal heard only insofar as a quorum of the board determined that their written statement disclosed a reasonable claim to refugee status.

26. For a detailed account of this process, see Gerald Dirks, "A Policy Within a Policy: The Identification and Admission of Refugees to Canada," *Canadian Journal of Political Science* 17 (1984): 283–85.

27. *Immigration Act, 1976*, S.C. 1976–77, c.52 ("Immigration Act"). All references are to the act as consolidated by R.S.C. 1985, c.I-2 as amended.

28. Memorandum to R. M. Tait, Assistant Deputy Minister (Special Projects), Department of Manpower and Immigration, from J. B. Bissett, Director General, Foreign Service Region, 13 August 1975, File 5780-1, at 3–4.

29. Memorandum to R. D. Jackson, Chief of Policy Analysis Group, Department of Manpower and Immigration, from J. L. Manion, Senior Assistant Deputy Minister, 19 June 1975, File 5882-3.

30. Letter to H. B. Robinson, Under-Secretary of State for External Affairs, from A. E. Gotlieb, Deputy Minister, Department of Manpower and Immigration, 20 July 1976, File 5882-7.

31. Memorandum to Members of the Legislative Drafting Group from J. Hucker, Department of Manpower and Immigration, 29 April 1976, File 5882-1.

32. It was argued that the incorporation of the Convention definition of refugee status would "reduce the litigation the Department is involved in and would facilitate public explanation of the new provisions on refugees": ibid.

33. A. E. Gotlieb, note 30 above.

34. Immigration Act, note 27 above, at s.3(g). This careful distinction between *legal obligations* (which are binding) and Canada's *humanitarian tradition* (which is only a guiding principle) reflects concerns within the Department of Manpower and Immigration about the use of overly broad language: J. L. Manion, note 29 above.

35. "[N]o person who is finally determined under this Act, or determined under the regulations, to be a Convention refugee . . . shall be removed from Canada to a country where the person's life or freedom would be threatened" unless the refugee was judged by the Minister to constitute a danger to the public or security of Canada: Immigration Act, note 27 above, at s.53(1) [formerly s.55].

36. See generally James Hathaway, *The Law of Refugee Status* (Toronto, 1991), 11–27.

37. J. B. Bissett, note 28 above, at 1–2.

38. Memorandum to L. E. Couillard, Deputy Minister from R. B. Curry, Assistant Deputy Minister (Immigration), 30 May 1969, File 5784-1.

39. *Regulations Respecting Admission and Removal from Canada of Persons Who Are Not Canadian Citizens*, S.O.R./78-172 ("Immigration Regulations"), at s.7.

40. "Any person who is a member of a class designated by the Governor in Council as a class, the admission of members of which would be in accordance with Canada's humanitarian tradition with respect to the displaced and the persecuted, may be granted admission": Immigration Act, note 27 above, at s.6(2).

41. *Regulations Respecting the Designation of Political Prisoners and Oppressed Persons Designated Class*, S.O.R./82-977. Since the class came into force in 1979, it has benefited persons from a variety of Central and South American countries, as well as from Poland. The innovation of this designated class is that it is applicable to persons still within their country of origin.

42. *Regulations Respecting the Designation of an Indochinese Designated Class,* S.O.R./78-931. Since 31 August 1990, Kampucheans are the only nationals included in this class: S.O.R./90-626. Moreover, as of 17 January 1991, members of this class must have arrived in Hong Kong, Thailand, Malaysia, Singapore, Indonesia, the Philippines, Korea, Taiwan, Japan, or Macao subsequent to 30 April 1975: S.O.R./91-111.

43. *Indochinese Designated Class (Transitional) Regulations,* S.O.R./90-627. Effective 17 January 1991, this class is restricted to Vietnamese and Laotians who arrived in Hong Kong before 16 June 1988; or in Thailand, Malaysia, Singapore, Indonesia, the Philippines, Korea, Taiwan, Japan, or Macao before 14 March 1989: S.O.R./91-112.

44. *Regulations Respecting the Designation of a Self-Exiled Persons Classs,* S.O.R./78-933. This class was abolished effective 31 August 1990: S.O.R./90-533.

45. R. B. Curry, note 38 above.

46. Employment and Immigration Canada, *Immigration Manual* (Ottawa, Minister of Supply and Services, 1990, as updated) at part I.S. 3.24(2)(a). These descriptions of the various designated classes (notes 41–44 above) contain similar provisions.

47. "Refugees who have been permanently resettled in another country are still entitled to the protection of the refugee Convention and Protocol. However, such persons are not to be selected in the refugee class for immigration to Canada unless they are facing persecution in their country of resettlement": Employment and Immigration Canada, note 46 above, at part I.S. 3.24(5)(a).

48. Officers abroad are required to ensure compliance with the general immigration requirements established by law: Employment and Immigration Canada, note 49 above, at part I.S. 3.24(6)(a). A series of "inadmissible classes" is prescribed by the Immigration Act, note 27 above, at s.19.

49. Specifically excluded are "persons who have been convicted of an offence that, if committed in Canada, constitutes or, if committed outside Canada, would constitute an offence . . . for which a maximum term of imprisonment of ten years or more may be imposed": Immigration Act, note 27 above, at s.19(1)(c).

50. Immigration Act, note 27 above, at s.19(1)(a)(ii). Officers abroad are directed to submit full details of medically inadmissible persons to Immigration headquarters "before a final decision is taken," as a recent policy change permits the admission of disabled refugees who, "following any necessary treatment or special assistance in Canada, . . . will be capable of successful establishment": Employment and Immigration Canada, note 46 above, at part I.S. 3.33(3) and (4).

51. Officers are directed to "take into consideration all of the factors used in assessing independent immigrants": Employment and Immigration Canada, note 46 above, at part I.S. 3.24(6).

52. Particularly important are the motivation and personal qualities essential to becoming established, and the adequacy of the applicant's education and training to ensure that "in the long term, the refugee will have the earning capacity to support his family and will not be dependent on welfare indefinitely": Employment and Immigration Canada, note 46 above, at section I.S. 3.24(6)(b).

53. "Canada is generous, Canada has been generous and the Minister has provided assurances that Canada will continue to be generous. But the [inland] determination system is not the be-all and end-all of Canada's generosity. It is one element, an important part of a totality that is exercised in many ways internal and external to Canada's immigration system": Raphael Girard, "Refugee Determination in Canada," in Alan Nash, ed., *Human Rights and the Protection of Refugees under International Law* (Halifax, 1988), 276. At the time, Mr. Girard was coordinator of Employment and Immigration Canada's Refugee Determination Task Force. See also text at note 62 below.

54. Employment and Immigration Canada, *Annual Report to Parliament: Immigration Plan for 1991–1995* (Ottawa and Hull, 1990), 10–11.

55. Ibid. at 11.

56. The government prepares an annual plan for resettlement of refugees from abroad via Canadian diplomatic posts. "Targets" are set for each of five geopolitical regions. The government argues that the process of fixing the allocations provides a flexible yet controlled response to refugee-producing situations as they evolve, and affords a means of reconciling percevied resettlement capacity with the actual extent of need abroad: Employment and Immigration Canada, *Canada's Refugee Strategy* (Ottawa and Hull, 1980), B1.

57. Immigration Regulations, note 39 above, at s.7(2).

58. Employment and Immigration Canada, note 54 above, at 9.

59. Ibid.

60. Ibid.

61. Employment and Immigration Canada, *Refugee Perspectives: 1987–1988* (Ottawa and Hull, 1987), 40.

62. Canada currently requires the nationals of more than one hundred countries to hold a visa in order to transit in or visit Canada. Included, for example, are China, El Salvador, Iran, Lebanon, Somalia, and Sri Lanka, all major sources of refugee flows into Canada: Immigration Regulations, note 39 above, at s.13(1) and Schedule II.

63. Raphael Girard, "Speaking Notes for an Address," Conference on Refuge or Asylum—A Choice for Canada, York University, 1986 (unpublished), at 4.

64. Immigration Act, note 27 above, at ss.2(1) and 19(1)(h).

65. See generally Erika Feller, "Carrier Sanctions and International Law," *International Journal of Refugee Law* 1 (1989): 48.

66. These programs are based on the authority to admit persons "for reasons of public policy or due to the existence of compassionate or humanitarian considerations": Immigration Act, note 27 above, at s.114(2) [formerly s.115(2)]. In 1985 and 1986, approximately 15 percent of total refugee acceptances were admitted to Canada pursuant to the special measures programs: Employment and Immigration Canada, note 61 above, at 40.

67. Removal orders were suspended in regard to the nationals of El Salvador, Iran, Lebanon, and Sri Lanka. Furthermore, eligible Chileans were only removed with the consent of National Immigration Headquarters: Employment and Immigration Canada, note 46 above, at part I.S. 26 (no longer in force).

68. Inland independent applications were permitted from the nationals of Chile, El Salvador, Guatemala, Iran, and Lebanon: Employment and Immigration Canada, note 46 above, at part I.S. 26 (no longer in force).

69. Special overseas sponsorship provisions are provided for the relatives of Canadians who are nationals of Chile, El Salvador, Guatemala, Lebanon, and Sri Lanka: Employment and Immigration Canada, *supra* note 46, at part I.S. 26.

70. Telex from Director General, Public Affairs, to all Canada Immigration Centers, 20 February 1987. "There will be about 2,000 admissions [per annum] from abroad through our special humanitarian programs. . . . They are admitted under the Assisted Relative category, and are assessed using relaxed selection criteria for humanitarian reasons": Employment and Immigration Canada, note 54 above, at 11.

71. *Re Singh and the Minister of Employment and Immigration,* [1985] 1 S.C.R. 177.

72. See generally James Hathaway, "Selective Concern: An Overview of Refugee Law in Canada," *McGill Law Journal* 33–34 (1988–89): 677 and 354.

73. Immigration Act, note 27 above, at s.90.1(1). This provision ceased to be in force on 1 July 1989.

74. Ibid., at s.46.01(1)(b).

75. Ibid., at s.94.2.

76. Ibid., at s.46.01.

77. "In effect, the legislation placed with Immigration Canada the management of the first-level determination process, making it difficult for the CRDD to control the pace and number of claims brought before it": Immigration and Refugee Board, *Annual Report for the Year Ending December 31, 1990* (Ottawa, 1991), 20.

78. Immigration and Refugee Board, "Notes for Remarks by Gordon Fairweather, Chairman, Immigration and Refugee Board, to the House of Commons Standing Committee on Labour, Employment and Immigration," 27 March 1991, at 2.

79. Immigration and Refugee Board, "News Release," 30 April 1991, at 2.

80. Immigration and Refugee Board, note 77 above, at 17.

81. See generally ibid. at 16.

82. Immigration and Refugee Board, "Notes for Remarks by Gordon Fairweather, Chairman, Immigration and Refugee Board, to the House of Commons Standing Committee on Labour, Employment and Immigration," 13 December 1990.

83. Immigration and Refugee Board, note 77 above, at 17–18.

84. Ibid., note 78 above, at 2–3.

85. Immigration Act, note 27 above, at s.82.3.

86. Ibid., at s.4(2.1).

87. Immigration and Refugee Board, *Annual Report for the Year Ending December 31, 1989* (Ottawa, 1990), 14; and Immigration and Refugee Board, note 77 above, at 18–19.

88. Immigration and Refugee Board, note 78 above, at 4–5.

89. Ibid., note 77 above, at 20.

90. See generally Hathaway, note 36 above. Of particular note are three recent decisions of the Federal Court of Appeal: *Joseph Adjei v. Minister of Employment and Immigration* (1989), 7 Imm. L.R. (2d) 169 (dealing with the standard of proof); *Vajie Salibian v. Minister of Employment and Immigration*, F.C.A.D. A-479-89, 24 May 1990 (establishing the eligibility of claims from situations of generalized oppression); and *Ahmad Ali Zalzali v. Minister of Employment and Immigration*, F.C.A.D. A-382-90, 30 April 1991 (in which the claims of persons from societies in which no effective government exists were held to be potentially within the scope of the Convention refugee definition).

91. See note 62.

92. "The relevant provisions of the *Immigration Act* represent a unilateral effort to deal with a sub-group of refugee claimants considered, *a priori*, to be some other State's responsibility. Even before the politically difficult and intrusive functions ever arose, of determining and listing which other friendly countries might be considered entirely or partially safe, this unilateral aspect probably destined the effort to failure": Law Reform Commission of Canada, *The Determination of Refugee Status in Canada: A Review of the Procedure: Preliminary Study: A Consultative Document* (Ottawa, 1991), 135.

93. "The fact that removals are not taking place to the extent authorized under the legislation means that there is still a 'pull' factor operating to draw people to this country under the guise of refugee claims": Immigration and Refugee Board, note 82 above, at 2.

94. See notes 28 and 53.

95. See generally Amnesty International, *Harmonization of Asylum Policy in Europe* (London, 1990); and H. Meijers, "Refugees in Western Europe: 'Schengen' Affects the Entire Refugee Law," *International Journal of Refugee Law* 2 (1990): 428.

96. Immigration and Refugee Board, note 79 above, at 4–5.

97. *Tractatenblad* 1985, 102.

98. *Convention Determining the State Responsible for Examining Applications for Asylum Lodged in one of the Member States of the European Communities*, reproduced in *Refugee Abstracts* 9 (1990): 66.

99. Employment and Immigration Canada, *Report on the Consultations on Immigration for 1991–1995* (Ottawa and Hull, 1990).

100. See note 90.

101. For example, during 1990 visa controls were in place for nine of the ten primary refugee source countries (Sri Lanka, Somalia, China, Bulgaria, Lebanon, El Salvador, Iran, Ghana, and Pakistan); Immigration Regulations, note 39 above, at s.13(1) and Schedule II; and Immigration and Refugee Board, note 77 above, at 20.

102. Law Reform Commission of Canada, note 92 above, at 136.

103. Ibid.

104. See generally James Hathaway, "A Reconsideration of the Underlying Premise of Refugee Law," *Harvard International Law Journal* 31 (1990): 129; Gervase Coles, "Approaching the Refugee Problem Tolday," in Gil Loescher and Laila Monahan, eds., *Refugees and International Relations* Oxford 1989), 373; and Jack Garvey, "Toward a Reformation of International Refugee Law," *Harvard International Law Journal* 26 (1985): 483.

PHILIP RUDGE

The Asylum Dilemma—Crisis in the Modern World: A European Perspective

The dark side of European history, the waves of persecution, the pogroms, and the explosions of political and ethnic violence have produced movements of refugees throughout the period of recorded history. There is nothing new in the phenomenon of forced displacement, of individuals and groups being suddenly uprooted and tragically torn from ties of nationality, of home, of family. One of the marks of social progress in Europe has been precisely the range of responses that have been developed to handle such movements of people, responses that have resulted in a codification of laws and the evolution of international institutions which, particularly in the twentieth century, constitute a remarkable example of internationalism and human solidarity. Such social progress has never been smooth; indeed it is disfigured by historical moments of great cruelty and shame where states have denied asylum to persons in acute distress. Worse, as the experience of Nazi Germany demonstrates, European states of immense sophistication and cultural richness have been capable of unspeakable savagery, which has led to the creation of enormous human displacements within Europe and beyond. Nevertheless, the right of asylum itself has become established as a norm of civilized international behavior in Europe and many millions of persecuted and marginalized people have benefited from it. Many millions more have within their family history an experience of someone who was forced to move, victimized by repression of their race, religion, their nationality, their opinions; and elsewhere, those who perished in ghettos, concentration camps, and unmarked killing fields.

In the last twenty to thirty years the need for asylum in Europe has also begun to be heard from non-Europeans, from survivors of persecution in

JOURNAL OF POLICY HISTORY, Vol. 4, No. 1, 1992.
Copyright © 1992 The Pennsylvania State University, University Park, PA.

Southeast Asia, Africa, and Latin America. The sea of misery and deprivation in Third World states that so often leads to persecution and grave violations of human rights is now lapping the shores of Europe. The refugee issue is now one that requires global responses, where European traditions of respect for human rights are being tested in terms both of the receiving policies of that region and of the contribution European states can make, individually and collectively, toward solving those crises that increasingly provoke forced migrations throughout the world. The decade of the 1990s has started with the numbers of persons seeking asylum in Europe running on a level unknown since the vast displacements following World War II (see Fig. 1 and Tables 2, 3, and 4). The financial costs governments are paying to process this historic movement are high. The asylum movements are also overshadowed by other non-refugee-related movements requiring separate treatment. There is governmental unease at the financial and social costs involved and widespread public ignorance and confusion about what is actually happening. In this disturbed and uncertain period, there is good reason to ask whether the principle of asylum can survive the immense pressures of the 1990s. My argument here is that indeed the right of asylum will prevail if it is based upon the correct principles, namely, those of a complex system of human rights observance developed by the international community in recent decades. It will not prevail if, instead, the governments of Europe opt for policies based on deterrence and restriction. This in turn depends on an understanding that "human rights" are not a soft, liberal notion promoted by well-meaning idealists, but a fundamental element in the resolution of the apalling problems that divide our world, at the center of which one so often finds the person who may no longer live in his or her own country and has to flee to seek a life of some security and dignity elsewhere.

I am writing not from a governmental point of view but from that of the nongovernmental advocate. The reason for this is simple. The Universal Declaration of Human Rights refers to human rights as a matter for the governments *and the peoples* of the world. While governments treat human rights matters alongside economic, diplomatic, and security concerns—sometimes, of course, to the severe detriment of human rights—the civil sector is constrained by the international response to universal human rights terms and agreements elaborated in our name by our governments and which must be invoked to measure the performance of the powerful toward the weak.

The right of asylum is an ancient right but also a fragile one that always has to be defended in the dialogue between government and civil society; it cannot be left to the realpolitik of the strong. In Europe in recent years

Fig. 1. Asylum-seekers in Europe.

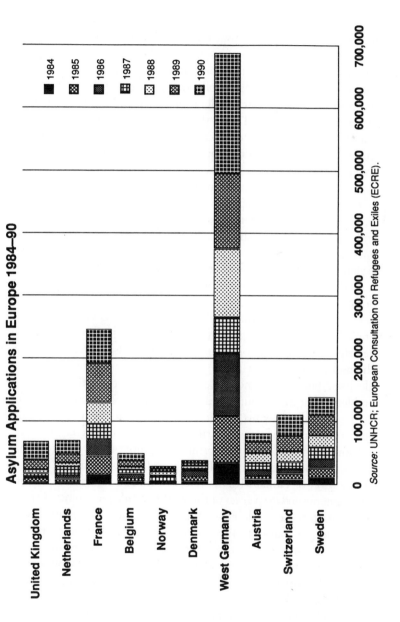

Asylum Applications in Europe 1984–90

1984
1985
1986
1987
1988
1989
1990

United Kingdom
Netherlands
France
Belgium
Norway
Denmark
West Germany
Austria
Switzerland
Sweden

0   100,000   200,000   300,000   400,000   500,000   600,000   700,000

Source: UNHCR; European Consultation on Refugees and Exiles (ECRE).

Table 1. Number of Asylum Applications in Europe, 1984–90

	1984	1985	1986	1987	1988	1989	1990[a]	Total
Sweden	11,300	15,000	15,000	18,100	19,500	30,335	30,000	139,235
Switzerland	7,400	9,700	8,500	10,900	16,326	23,193	35,836	111,855
Austria	7,400	6,700	8,700	11,400	15,233	18,252	14,110	81,795
West Germany	34,400	73,900	99,700	57,400	108,076	121,434	193,063	687,973
Denmark	4,300	8,700	9,300	2,750	4,668	4,558	5,292	39,568
Norway	400	800	2,700	8,600	6,600	4,433	3,962	27,495
Belgium	4,000	6,300	7,500	6,000	4,855	8,200	13,000	49,855
France	16,100	28,900	26,300	24,800	34,352	61,372	56,053	247,877
Netherlands	2,600	5,700	5,900	13,450	7,486	13,898	21,208	70,242
United Kingdom	3,900	5,500	3,900	4,500	5,263	15,530	30,000	68,593
Total	91,800	161,200	187,500	157,900	222,359	301,205	402,524	1,524,488

[a]Provisional figure only for Sweden, Belgium, and the United Kingdom; first nine months only for Austria.
Source: UNHCR; European Consultation on Refugees and Exiles (ECRE).

Table 2. Asylum Applications, Population, GNP, and Size in Europe, 1984–90

	Population (millions)	Average Number of Asylum-seekers per Year	Average Number of Asylum-seekers per Millions Inhabitants per Year	Per caput GNP (U.S.$)	Per caput GNP Average Number of Asylum-seekers per Year	Population per sq km	Average Number of Asylum-seekers per sq km per year
Sweden	8.50	19,891	2,340	21,700	9.27	18.90	.04
Switzerland	6.60	15,989	2,423	32,825	13.55	159.80	.30
Austria[a]	7.60	12,356	1,626	18,325	11.27	90.60	.13
West Germany	61.50	98,281	1,598	21,975	13.75	247.30	.33
Denmark	5.10	5,652	1,108	23,300	21.02	118.40	.13
Norway	4.20	3,927	935	23,425	25.05	12.90	.01
Belgium	9.90	7,122	719	16,675	23.18	324.30	.20
France	56.10	35,411	631	18,500	29.31	103.10	.06
Netherlands	14.90	10,034	673	17,450	25.91	362.00	.20
United Kingdom	57.30	9,799	171	14,375	84.06	234.10	.03

[a]Average number of asylum-seekers based on 1990 projection.
Source: UNHCR; *The Economist*; World Bank; European Consultation on Refugees and Exiles (ECRE).

Table 3. Refugees in Relation to Indigenous Population and GNP per Caput, 1989

Host Country	Population (millions)	Number of Refugees	Ratio of Refugees to Population	GNP per caput (U.S. $)
Jordan	4.10	908,000	1:4	1,420
Lebanon	3.30	295,000	1:10	N/K
Malawi	8.70	823,000	1:10	190
Iran	53.90	2,710,000	1:20	4,120
Somalia	8.20	350,000	1:23	280
Pakistan	110.40	3,783,600	1:29	380
Swaziland	.80	24,800	1:32	750
Sudan	24.50	749,500	1:33	350
Syria	12.20	275,000	1:44	2,730
Sweden	8.50	139,800	1:60	21,700
France	56.10	184,500	1:304	18,500
United Kingdom	57.30	101,300	1:566	14,375

Sources: UNHCR; World Bank; U.S. Committee for Refugees; European Consultation on Refugees and Exiles (ECRE).

there has been a growing divergence in the analysis of the refugee and asylum challenge between the governments on the one hand, and the civil human rights community on the other. While that distinction is necessary and often highly desirable, the polarization has often taken forms that do not lead to good policy, and there is evidently a need to find ways of agreeing on a common agenda to make any progress.

Background

Looking at the global refugee picture in the early 1990s, it is clear that the crisis is not one that affects so much the affluent and relatively peaceful European world but rather one that adds to the intense strains upon the poorer and less secure states. Nonetheless, it is important to remember that Europe has in the past been characterized by massive movements of people. Indeed, in living memory Europe has witnessed the greatest human displacements in the history of the continent. According to some estimates, as many as 60 million people were displaced by the catastrophic events of World War II. And in the longer perspective of history, European states have witnessed refugees on the move in substantial numbers. Many date the modern history of displacement to just five hundred years ago, when in 1492 the first expulsions took place of the Jews from Spain. In the following two centuries more than a million refugees could be found moving through Europe. What is characteristic of these early refugee groups is that in general they were members of religious minorities, be they the Jews expelled from Spain or, later, protestants from France and the Spanish Netherlands, and later various protestant groups whose freedom of religious expression was repressed in Scandinavia in the eighteenth century. Naturally, before the development of the nation-states in the eighteenth and nineteenth centuries, these movements of persons were not a matter for governmental responsibilities as such, but rather the refugees resolved their difficulties through processes of local integration or through the intervention of local leaders and benevolent patrons. The concept of international systems of responsibility for protection and assistance, let alone the holding center or refugee camp, were unknown until relatively recent times. Even the term "refugee" as such, insofar as it was used before the nineteenth century, almost exclusively referred to the protestants who were forced out of France following the revocation of the Edict of Nantes at the end of the seventeenth century. Only at the very end of the eighteenth century, for example, did the *Encylopedia Britannica* contain an expanded description of the term to apply not only to the French protestants but also to "such as leave their country in time of distress, and hence, since the revolt of the British colonies in America we have frequently heard of American Refugees."

The growing consciousness in European society of the phenomenon of the refugee as a factor in international relations is, however, a phenomenon only of the last hundred years. It was given a great impetus by the immense movements of Jews from Imperial Russia at the end of the nineteenth and the beginning of the twentieth century. In the years just before the conflagration of World War I, more than two and a half million refugees are thought to have moved west. The hideous suffering and devastation of the war itself served to displace many millions more. In the aftermath of the war, when European statesmen met to redraw the map of Europe, it was evident that the new political boundaries would find substantial minorities of people living under the control of governments to which they found they had little allegiance. Thus the reordering of populations in the new political configuration inevitably provoked further substantial movements of people in the 1920s. A key moment in consolidating international cooperation to deal with the problem came with the decision of the League of Nations to establish a High Commission for refugees and appoint as its first chief the Norwegian Friedthof Nansen, who served until his death in 1930. Despite immense problems, practical and political, too few resources, and many conflicts between states, Nansen and his High Commission made a major contribution to creating the sine qua non without which solutions to the refugee crises are impossible, namely, political will. His greatest monument was the so-called Nansen Passport, a document that gave juridical recognition of international responsibility for the protection of refugees.

While the League of Nations intended that the High Commission's work should be of limited duration, events in Germany in the 1930s soon made it clear that new and different refugee flows would demand the attention of the world, and especially of Western European states. The horrors of anti-Semitism and the racial-purity ideology of the Nazi regime in the 1930s meant growing outflows of victims from Central Europe, some of which, to our lasting shame, provoked hostility and anti-Semitism among the potential receiving states, so much as that an unknown number of Jews perished through their failure to obtain access to safety beyond the reaches of the German fascist state. The apotheosis of the Nazi experiment and its lust for military domination that culminated in World War II produced displacements on a scale never before seen in Europe. It also resulted in profound shock to European notions of self-esteem. The horror and revulsion felt by many governments and public opinion in the immediate postwar period—the sense of "never again"—did, however, produce a series of initiatives of immense significance for the development of international responsibility that we now, in the 1990s, take for granted. In the few years immediately following the end of the war in 1945, this new feeling found its finest expression in the creation by the international community of institutions mandated to regularize relations between states in the human rights field, including the matter of treating refugees with dignity and shared responsibility. In addition to the United Nations Relief and Rehabilitation Administration (UNRRA), 1946 saw the creation of the International Refugee Organization (IRO) and 1950 the United Nations High Commission for Refugees (UNHCR).

While the founding of the IRO as an instrument for collective humanitarian action was bedeviled from the start by profound ideological differences between the Western powers and those under Soviet influence, nonetheless it did manage to create a remarkable degree of East-West consensus on groups of displaced persons in Europe who were deemed of common concern, and in particular it clarified some important principles on the basis of which any individual could object to being repatriated. In language that anticipated the terminology eventually used in the the "classic" Geneva 1951 Convention definition, the IRO laid out as legitimate grounds for an individual to refuse repatriation as "persecution or

fear, based on reasonable grounds, of persecution because of race, religion, nationality or political opinion." When the UNHCR replaced the
IRO with a more global mandate, the deepening Cold War divisions cast
a shadow over the notion of universalizing international responsibility for
refugees, particularly as the vast majority of the asylum-seekers in Western Europe for the next thirty years were from the Soviet bloc. The
suspicions underlying the ideological divide meant that for much if its life
UNHCR has been seen very much as an instrument of Western states; it
is one of the many positive consequences of the changes in the Soviet
Union from 1985 onward that gradually this wall of hostility to UNHCR
has been broken down, so that now in the 1990s the organization is being
actively consulted on the management of the new forced migrations occurring in Central and Eastern Europe.

Nonetheless, since 1945 the divisions of Europe have been profound,
and the rivalries of power groups and the creation of separate economic
blocs have meant that many areas of social and humanitarian policy have
been handled not only as a matter of internal national policy by a variety
of European institutions at all political levels. Those seeking asylum must
first and foremost still confront the demands of the sovereign nation-
states of Europe; at the regional level the twelve states of the European
Community are increasingly engaged in devising policies affecting refugee
and asylum rights and provisions; the twenty-five-member Council of
Europe has since 1949 also played a significant role in developing the
governing European human rights framework in many areas, including
those dealing with the treatment of refugees and asylum-seekers; and most
recently the thirty-eight nation Conference on Security and Cooperation
in Europe (CSCE), which brings together all states of the European
continent with the United States and Canada, has committed itself to
expanding the "Human Dimension" of the so-called Common European
Home. In the December 1990 Paris Charter all these states for the first
time in recent history committed themselves to the promotion of a detailed range of agreed human rights principles for all legal residents within
their territories.

The upshot is that for the would-be student of these matters there is not
only the single geographical concept of "Europe," but there is also a
European space of intersecting political and economic interest groups,
some of which are increasingly harmonizing important areas of social
policy. The new era that Europe has entered since the demise of the
dominant ideology in Central and Eastern Europe at the end of the 1980s
has raised hopes of greater respect for human rights throughout the continent, but at the same time it was revealed a resurgence of nationalism,

triumphalism, and the outbreak of religious and ethnic hatreds. Furthermore, the new Europe is badly disfigured by immense differences in economic and social circumstances; in some areas the risk of major economic
collapse and breakdown in order add to the pressures on people to move,
not necessarily or normally for reasons related to a well-founded fear of
persecution, but through overwhelming hopelessness and despair of im-
provements in their expectations in the area of economic, social, and
cultural rights. All these factors, together with the substantially rising
numbers of persons applying for asylum from outside Europe, mean that
the treatment of refugees and asylum-seekers in the early 1990s is problematic, involving great stresses on the national determination procedures, a
rising risk of summary rejection at borders and of *refoulement*, disorder in
intergovernmental relations, and a growing pressure to develop and harmonize restrictive and deterrent legislation to "control" the situation. The
heartbreak and insecurity this disorder inevitably brings to the refugees
seeking sanctuary is growing proportionately.

Problems of Understanding

One of the problems in discussing the refugee and asylum policies in
Europe is the degree of confusion and misrepresentation, deliberate or
otherwise, about the nature of the movements we are witnessing. Clearly
good policy-making, especially in the human rights area, where failure
can have grave human consequences, depends on an accurate analysis of
the phenomenon that the policy-making is intended to treat. It is not
only in the lesser-quality newspapers or in the mouth of racists and xeno-
phobes that one witnesses such misrepresentation; it is unfortunately all
too prevalent at the official level, where the refugee issue collapses into
other issues, where the human rights dimension is lost sight of, and where
the rights of asylum-seekers are decided in the same basket as such threats
to our societies as terrorism. It is extraordinary but true that even in the
last decade of the twentieth century it is still necessary to restate the
obvious: that at its root and in its evolution the refugee question is
fundamentally a human rights issue. The crisis for the refugee starts in
countries that are unwilling (and indeed often unable, due to crucifying
social pressures) to honor even the minimum human rights. How people
driven from their countries are received and treated in exile is a matter of
the human rights policies of European states. And of course how such
persons may eventually and voluntarily return home has important human rights implications. It is logically impossible to separate the refugee

question from the overall human rights context, or indeed from the nexus
of issues related to issues of peaceful and sustainable development.

Here are two particularly graphic demonstrations of the failure to put
the refugee issue in the correct perspective. It is often said in official
circles that the refugee situation has fundamentally changed. This kind of
assertion must be treated with immense care, to study the interplay of
foreign-policy and domestic pressures on asylum policy, to review the
development of the jurisprudence, and to compare one country with
another. If one does this, then the following picture emerges, namely,
that today, as in the past, people continue to flee to (Western) Europe
from human rights violations, from generalized repression, from civil
wars, from armed conflict, and from extreme violence. Today as in the
past some refugees are more welcome than others; today as in the past
some refugees are able to resolve their problems near home, while others
have to travel substantial distances to get the protection they need. This
is not to deny that there are (and must be in a changing world) several
new factors that have an effect on the refugee situation. Among these are,
for exmaple, the greater availability of long-range transportation, which
facilitates transcontinental movements, and the new information order,
which on the one hand brings far more human suffering into our consciousness and under our responsibility, and on the other transmits the
realities of our safer, peaceful, and more prosperous Europe to the most
dangerous and oppressive regions of the world. The principal complicat-
ing factor in the European refugee picture in recent years, however, is the
movement of persons for reasons that are not directly related to persecution or the violation of fundamental civil and political rights. Since most
European countries imposed a halt on immigration after the oil crisis of
1972, these movements have grown and so far states have not devised a
mechanism to handle them. What has ensued is an unpleasant character-
ization of virtually all asylum-seekers as "merely economic migrants" or as
abusers of the system. Most nongovernmental opinion takes the view that
it is the failure of states to develop policies in the area of immigration that
is threatening the asylum system rather than massive abuse, but this
misrepresentation nonetheless has gained wide currency and complicates
the discussion of an appropriate human rights-based response.

A second illustration of the problem of representation is the way in
which states refer to their low refugee recognition rate as proof that
asylum-seekers are merely motivated by economic reasons. On so many
occasions UNHCR, the Council of Europe, and many legal and human
rights bodies have been driven to point out that a number of European
governments have in fact changed their behavior as regards the implemen-

tation of the Geneva Convention so that now it is used in an excessively illiberal and restrictive manner. The notion, in other words, that there was some golden age of "pure" refugees in the 1950s and 1960s that is now tarnished by abuse is simply nonsense.

The Policy Response

Given the difficulties just described, the question arises whether the policies devised by governments are appropriate to the situation. The question is a vital one and the answer may perhaps be judged by two crucial standards: first, are states acting toward refugees and asylum-seekers in the light of the obligations that they have freely entered into by signing human rights conventions and agreements? and second, do the actions of states at present serve to strengthen or to undermine the international solidarity with countries of the world where the principal refugee crises are occurring? Generalizations are of course dangerous, but some pointers for further analysis can be given, and evidence can be cited that relates both to the method and content of the policy-making.

In terms of the *method*, asylum and refugee policies are now on the agendas of an extraordinary number of official policy-making groups, consultations, committees, secretariats, working groups, and organizations in Europe. This explosion of political interest, however, has not been accompanied by an increase in openness and transparency in the policy-making. It is widely felt that the more important the work, the more secretive the process, and the evidence is clear that regarding the formulation of some of the most crucial new conventions many European governments have opted to entrust the drafting work to confidential and secretive groups rather than to have a full, open debate. Regarding the three key instruments recently devised that bear on the refugee issue—the Schengen Treaty, the 1990 Dublin Convention, determining the country responsible for examining an asylum request, and the 1991 draft convention on crossing external frontiers—have been carried on largely behind closed doors. Even UNHCR has been substantially marginalized in the process. Contrary to the general trend of human rights legislation since 1945 toward openness and consultation, the European states have approached the law-making task regarding refugees and asylum-seekers from an administrative and bureaucratic direction with little regard to the special human rights requirements. In addition, they have entrusted the work to centralized bureaucracies with little democratic scrutiny or parliamentary control.

The twelve states of the European Community will establish their unified market for the free movement of goods, services, and capital by the end of 1992. Insofar as the harmonization measures of the Single European Act will also directly concern the movements of peoples into and within the European Community, we are dealing not with abstract administrative exercises but with matters of direct consequence for asylum-seekers. If European states are worried about potential large-scale asylum movements from the developing world, there must be better ways of handling such movements in conformity with the Geneva Convention and International burden-sharing than by secretive processes driven by the requirements of economic model-makers.

As a result, the new legislation has attracted much criticism and real alarm in many circles. On the Schengen Convention, the Dublin Convention, and the draft treaty on the crossing of external frontiers, nongovernmental organizations have asked a number of questions to see if the authorities can prove that these treaties do not violate the Geneva Convention and other human rights obligations, or indeed, the very right to seek asylum itself. The critique is a far-reaching one and involves among other things:

- Concern that access to the territory of the European Community may be denied to those who need asylum.
- Concern that these treaties are inflexible and ignore the specific legal and social character of the refugee and asylum-seeker.
- Concern that sensitive data may not be protected by the enormous expansion of electronic data collection envisaged in these treaties.
- Anxiety about the impact of sanctions on transport companies and about certain visa policies that throw unreasonable responsibilities on commercial agents and threaten the chance for persecuted individuals even to get out of their country.
- Confusion about the implementation mechanisms of these Conventions and the absence of UNHCR involvement.
- Concern at the lack of legal redress against breaches of the Conventions because they are not part of European Community Law or subject to the Luxembourg Court.

Where to Go from Here?

The need for open, informed consultative policy-making is self-evident in democratic societies. In terms of approach and content, current European policy-making is unsatisfactory, especially as it does not command the support of a large group of people with knowledge and experience in the field. So two questions arise: What institutional arrangements would improve the situation, and what should be the priority agenda? As the issue assumes greater urgency on the political agenda, the existing machinery is showing itself to be inadequate to the task. At the United Nations level the refugee question will increasingly be a matter for the redefinition of responsibilities under the so-called new international humanitarian order. European states are actively involved in these discussions, both in terms of strengthening assistance to countries of first asylum and in rethinking developmental options. But on the European regional level there are serious gaps in the discussion of European asylum policy and in the development of approaches to more global issues. The many bodies referred to above are indeed active, but all too often they take a short-term protectionist approach. A number of new initiatives are currently spoken of in this regard. At a major joint governmental-NGO conference held in the Hague in December 1989, a proposal was made to set up a European Asylum Commission, or something similar, preferably within the Council of Europe. The terms of reference of this body were described as follows: "Problems related to asylum seekers and refugees should be discussed at regular intervals by a consultative committee composed of European governments, UNHCR and other intergovernmental organisations and representatives of NGO coordinations established at national and European level. The consultative committee would deal with asylum policy in Europe and with refugee policy world wide on the basis of the application of Human Rights principles." The Council of Europe itself, comprising as it does twenty-five member states with a distinguished history in human rights work, has suggested a series of roundtables to bring together politicians, senior legal and academic people, and representatives of international humanitarian organizations, whose work would be prepared at the technical level by experts and consultants. The objective would be to present concrete proposals for policy action to be decided on the basis of a thorough examination of all legal and political aspects of the present situation.

There is growing pressure on the Conference on Security and Cooperation in Europe (CSCE) to take the refugee issue on board as part of its declared objective to bring all the European states into a regular human rights framework. The Paris Charter of 1990 is a document of extraordinary significance, signaling a major commitment to intensify human rights work within the framework of the CSCE. Accordingly, 1990 saw the establishment of the CSCE Conflict Prevention Secretariat in Vienna, the Secretariat for the elections in Warsaw, and the overall Secretariat in Prague. The year 1992 will see the start of the new CSCE

Parliamentary Assembly. While regular mechanisms do not yet exist to treat the refugee issue within these new institutional structures, the political potential there is great and can only increase in the future. So far as one can anticipate future refugee movements from Central and Eastern Europe, it may be that they will be the result of unresolved ethnic and religious conflicts, and so there is an excellent chance to look at the problem and use early warning and conciliation techniques that are part of the CSCE institutionalization.

However these institutional arrangements develop, urgent attention will be required to harmonize practices and standards for the treatment of asylum-seekers and refugees within the European states themselves. Beyond the basic question of addressing the humanitarian needs of the individual and the requirements of good legal and administrative processes, there is a fundamental inconsistency in the present situation: that while the processes of harmonization of border controls and access to the territory are now quite advanced, there is no comparable harmonization of the criteria whereby asylum claims are assessed. The jurisprudence on asylum claims differs substantially from country to country, and yet under the provisions of the Schengen and Dublin conventions, states are required to accept the decisions of other states. This could mean, for example, that an asylum-seeker might have received a positive decision in one signatory state of the Convention but a negative one in another, and under the new rules the negative will normally stand if that is the first and only decision made.

It is also the case that in the supposedly "harmonized" European Community the conditions under which asylum-seekers are required to live in the different countries of Europe vary enormously. Indeed, on a host of critical questions agreement is lacking between states. A few illustrations will make the point.

Fair and efficient procedures for the determination of refugee status. Throughout history refugee numbers rise and fall, and it is clear that European states have not adapted their asylum procedures to the increasing numbers of asylum applications. There has been a lot of discussion about "accelerated procedures." Recently NGOs have suggested how to establish a regime of fair and efficient procedures that will try to balance the asylum-seekers' right to the strongest legal safeguards with the need to make decisions swiftly and efficiently. A number of detailed proposals have been made, including one that might separate the manifestly well-founded and manifestly unfounded claims from the general caseload so as to concentrate resources on the complex cases that need further examination.

State Practices at frontiers and airports. At the Council of Europe Colloquy on *Human Rights Without Frontiers* in December 1989, a number of states elaborated how standards should evolve. Yet, since then, little has been done to implement recommendations relating to practices at frontiers. With the intensification of cooperation between policing and immigration officials at the strengthened external frontier of the European Community, it will be essential to ensure that the highest legal and procedural standards are maintained at this critical moment in the movement of the person seeking asylum. The risks of *refoulement* will otherwise be substantially heightened.

The arrival of undocumented asylum-seekers. A major irritant for many Western governments is the arrival of asylum-seekers without any kind of identification papers or with false documents. Often refugees have to flee their country as a matter of life or death and obviously cannot avail themselves of the bureaucratic requirements that govern the movements of the rest of us. Absurdly, the very measures that were introduced in the 1980s to counter this practice actually exacerbated the problem. The targeting of visas and the punishing of airlines have led directly to refugees being forced to obtain false papers in order to leave their country of persecution and seek asylum in a safe country. This is a classic case where the technocratic response in fact fails to address the seriousness of the issue with sensitivity and flexibility. The problem is by no means simple, but the solution lies in removing the obstacles, by improving the fairness and efficency of procedures, and by paying closer attention to the problems arising in the area of origin of the asylum-seekers.

The enormous differences in the social provisions for refugees and asylum-seekers in the different states of Europe naturally reflect the economic and social standards of the indigenous populations. But if states wish to remove the push-and-pull factors that to some extent determine where asylum-seekers try to establish themselves, they will need to take note that housing, health, social benefits, and family reunion policies are seriously inconsistent. Most important perhaps in this regard is the position of persons permitted to stay in European countries but who are not recognized under the Geneva Convention. These persons inhabit a twilight world possessing only rudimentary rights.

In the new situation in Europe following the collapse of the ideological order in Central and Eastern Europe, there is a growing concern about the possible creation of new refugee flows from the ethnic and religious conflicts that are once again surfacing. There is also a feeling that these newly democratizing states will have to take their share of the responsibility of accepting and intergrating refugees on their own territories from within the region and from further afield rather than simply continuing their traditional role as places of transit to the West. While stories of millions of "refugees" on the move have proved hysterical, nonetheless there are reasons to expect significant migration of a principally economic nature, which in itself may put pressure on the refugee and asylum processing systems. Therefore, it is important to watch the response of the Western European states to the political disintegration in some Central European states and their response to the economic, cultural, and political requirements for peaceful and sustainable development there. The European Community is the key to this process through the consolidation of the immense wealth, political experience, and economic strength of its member states. There is of course a natural concern that preoccupations with events in Central and Eastern Europe will reduce the traditional solidarity with the developing countries. In other words, more for the East could mean less for the South. But from the point of view of a long-term refugee policy in the "Common European Home," it is important to question what kind of assistance is being made available to the East. At present and overwhelmingly, the interest of West European governments seems to be with the development of the free-market economies and with economic institution building. This ultimately will prove to be a rather sterile policy if it is divorced from the wider requirements of democratization. The challenge is an obvious one—namely, whether social regeneration should happen across the social political and cultural spectrum, whether a dynamic civil society is encouraged, and whether the new human rights and democratic challenges facing those countries are met by an informed, trained, and active civil sector. In practical terms, two basic needs will have to be addressed: (1) the training of individuals who will be involved in the treatment of refugees in that region and who will be required to implement the provision of the human rights and humanitarian law conventions that those states are becoming party to; and (2) institution building so that a strong and active civil society can develop, with nongovernmental and people's organizations playing an active part in deepening the democratic functioning in the area.

A great deal has been written recently about the root cause of refugee movements, both within Europe and, more important, elsewhere in the world, as well as the actions required to address these root causes. Experience makes one less hopeful about the real commitment behind the rhetoric, and the genuine intention of states to undertake radical transformations in their international behavior, which will be required if we are to address the problems that derive from the grotesque inequalities and the structural poverty of our world. What is required is much greater engagement by the democratic institutions of Europe in a process that will be increasingly vital in the treatment of situations that generate refugee movements. This is work in the field of negotiation of conflict, and in techniques of conciliation and reconciliation.

There are refugee situations in the world where a combination of early warning and of conciliation and externalization of the conflict between parties may make the problem far more susceptible to treatment than the traditional root-cause analysis. Quiet ad hoc diplomacy is not enough; something more structured is needed. In the post–Cold War era, the United Nations has been revitalized as an instrument of peacekeeping and peacemaking. The United Nations has sponsored agreements in Namibia, Cambodia, El Salvador, and the Western Sahara, to name only a few examples. There have also been bilateral and regional peace initiatives to resolve conflicts, halt military coups, and respond to other refugee-inducing events in Ethiopia, Liberia, Haiti, and Yugoslavia. While not all of these initiatives have been successful, the international community must build on this experience and actively mobilize new ideas and imagination for the resolution of what often appear to be intractable problems.

Recommended Reading and Sources

Aga Khan, Sadruddin. *Legal Problems Related to Refugees and Displaced Persons.* The Hague: Academy of International Law, 1976.

———. *Study on Human Rights and Massive Exoduses.* ECOSOC doc. E/CN 4/1503, 1981.

———. "Towards a Humanitarian World Order." *Third World Affairs* (1985): 105–23.

Aleinikoff, T. Alexander. "Political Asylum in the Federal Republic of Germany and Republic of France: Lessons for the United States." *University of Michigan Journal of Law Reform* 17 (Winter 1984): 183–241.

———, and Martin, David. *Immigration: Process and Policy.* St. Paul, Minn.: West Publishing Co., 1985.

Anker, Deborah E., et al. *The Law of Asylum in the United States: A Manual for Practitioners and Adjudicators.* Washington, D.C.: American Immigration Lawyers Association, 1989.

Avery, Christopher. "Refugee Status Decision-Making in Ten Countries." *Stanford Journal of International Law* 17 (Winter 1984): 183–241.

Beyer, Gregg. "Improving International Response to Humanitarian Situations." Washington, D.C.: Refugee Policy Group, 1987.

Bramwell, Anna (ed.). *Refugees in the Age of Total War.* London: Unwin Hyman, 1988.

Brown, Francis J. (ed.). *Refugees.* Special Issue of Annals of the American Academy of Political and Social Science, 203 (1936).

Carlin, James L. "The Development of U.S. Refugee and Migration Policies: An International Context." *Journal of Refugee Resettlement* 1 (August 1981): 9–14.

Cels, Johan. *A Liberal and Humane Policy for Refugees and Asylum Seekers: Still a Realistic Option?* London: European Consultation on Refugees and Exiles, 1986.

Center for Migration Studies. *International Migration Review.* Journal of human migration and refugee movements. Staten Island, N.Y.: CMS. Quarterly.

Cohen, Roberta. *Introducing Refugee Issues into the United Nations Human Rights Agenda.* Washington, D.C.: Refugee Policy Groups, 1990.

Coles, Gervase J. L. *Solutions to the Problem of Refugees and the Protection of Refugees: A Background Study.* Geneva: UNHCR, 1989.

———. *Voluntary Repatriation: A Background Study.* For Roundtable on Voluntary Repatriation [San Remo: International Institute of Humanitarian Law]. Geneva: UNHCR, July 1985.

Crisp, Jeff. "Refugee Repatriation: New Pressures and Problems." *Migration World* 14 (1987).

D'Souza, Frances, and Jeff Crisp. *The Refugee Dilemma.* Minority Rights Group Report No. 43. London: Minority Rights Group. February 1985.

de Zayas, Alfred M. *Nemesis at Potsdam: The Anglo-Americans and Expulsions of the Germans*. London: Routledge and Kegan Paul, 1979.

Dinnerstein, Leonard. *America and the Survivors of the Holocaust, 1941–1945*. New York: Columbia University Press, 1982.

Donnelly, Jack. "International Human Rights: A Regime Analysis." *International Organization* 40 (Summer 1985): 249–70.

Dowty, Alan. *Closed Borders: The Contemporary Assault on Freedom of Movement*. New Haven: Yale University Press, 1987.

Drüke, L. *Preventive Action for Refugee-Producing Situations*. Frankfurt am Main and New York: Peter Lang, 1990.

Elliot, Mark. *Pawns of Yalta*. Champaign: University of Illinois Press, 1982.

Fagen, Patricia Weiss, and Susan Forbes. *Safe Haven Options in Industrialized Countries*. Washington, D.C.: Refugee Policy Group, 1987.

Federal Republic of Germany Interministerial Working Group. *Refugee Concept*. Bonn: Federal Ministry of the Interior. 25 September 1990.

Ferris, Elizabeth G. *Central American Refugees and the Politics of Protection*. New York: Praeger, 1987.

———. "The Politics of Asylum: Mexico and the Central American Refugees." *Journal of Inter-American Studies and World Affairs* 26 (August 1984): 357–84.

——— (ed.). *Refugees and World Politics*. New York: Praeger, 1985.

Forbes, Martin S. "Emigration, Immigration and Changing East-West Relations." Issue Paper. Washington, D.C.: Refugee Policy Group. November 1989.

Forsythe, David P. "The United Nations and Human Rights, 1945–1985." *Political Science Quarterly* 100 (Summer 1985): 249–70.

Gallagher, Dennis (ed.). "Refugees: Issues and Directions." *International Migration Review* 20 (Summer 1986).

———, Susan Forbes, and Patricia Weiss Fagen. *Of Special Humanitarian Concern: U.S. Refugee Admissions since Passage of the Refugee Act*. Washington, D.C.: Refugee Policy Group, 1985.

Ghoshal, Animesh, and Thomas M. Crowley. "Refugees and Immigrants: A Human Rights Dilemma." *Human Rights Quarterly* 5 (August 1983): 327–47.

Gibney, Mark (ed). *Open Borders? Closed Societies? The Ethical and Political Questions*. Westport, Conn.: Greenwood Press, 1988.

——— (ed.). *World Justice? U.S. Courts and International Human Rights*. Boulder, Colo.: Westview Press, 1991.

Golden, Ronny, and Michael McConnell. *Sanctuary: The New Underground Railroad*. Maryknoll, N.Y.: Orbis Books, 1986.

Goodwin-Gill, G. *The Refugee in International Law*. Oxford: Clarendon Press, 1983.

Gordenker, Leon. *Refugees in International Politics*. London: Croom Helm, 1987.

Grahl-Madsen, Atle. *The Status of Refugees in International Law*, 2 vols. Leiden: A.W. Sijthoff, 1966, 1972.

Hakovirta, Harto. *Territorial Asylum*. Dobbs Ferry, N.Y.: Oceana Publications, 1980.

———. *Third World Conflicts and Refugeeism: Dimensions, Dynamics and Trends of the World Refugee Problem*. Helsinki: The Finnish Society of Sciences and Letters, 1986.

Hanson, Christopher T. "Behind the Paper Curtain: Asylum Policy v. Asylum Practice." *New York University Review of Law and Social Change* 7 (Winter 1978), 107–41.

Harmonization of Asylum Policy in Europe. London: Amnesty International. 17 April 1990.

Harrell-Bond, Barbara E. "Repatriation: Under What Conditions Is It the Most Desirable Solution for Refugees? An Agenda for Research." *African Studies Review* 31 (1988).

Hathaway, James. *The Law of Refugee Status*. Toronto: Butterworths, 1991.

———. "Reconceiving Refugee Law as Human Rights Protection." *Journal of Refugee Studies* 4 (1991): 113–31.

———. "Selective Concern: An Overview of Refugee Law in Canada." *McGill Law Journal* 33 (1988): 474–515.

———. "A Reconsideration of the Underlying Premise of Refugee Law." *Harvard International Law Journal* 31 (1990): 129–83.

Häusermann, J. *Root Causes of Displacement: The Legal Framework for International Concern and Action.* London: Rights and Humanity, 1986.

Helton, Arthur. "The Legality of Detaining Refugees in the United States." *Review of Law and Social Change* 14 (New York University, 1986).

———. "Political Asylum under the 1980 Refugee Act: An Unfulfilled Promise." *University of Michigan Journal of Law Reform* 17 (1984): 243.

Hewlett, Sylvia Ann. "Coping with Illegal Immigrants." *Foreign Affairs* 60 (Winter 1981–82): 358–78.

Holborn, Louise. *The International Refugee Organization: A Specialized Agency of the United Nations, Its History and Work, 1946–52.* London: Oxford University Press, 1956.

———. *Refugees, A Problem of Our Time: The Work of the United Nations High Commissioner for Refugees,* 2 vols. Metuchen, N.J.: Scarecrow Press, 1975.

Hull, Elizabeth. *Without Justice for All.* Westport, Conn.: Greenwood Press, 1985.

Humphrey, Derek, and Michael Ward. *Passports and Politics.* London: Penguin Books, 1974.

Intergovernmental Committee for Migration and the Research Group for European Migration Problems. *International Migration.* Review on the role of migratory movements in the contemporary world in English/French/Spanish. Geneva: ICM. Quarterly.

International Bibliography of Refugee Literature. Geneva: International Refugee Integration Resource Center, 1985.

International Journal of Refugee Law. Oxford: Oxford University Press. Quarterly.

Interpreter Releases. Information service on asylum, immigration, naturalization, and related matters. Washington, D.C.: Federal Publications. Weekly.

Jaeger, Gilbert. *Status and International Protection of Refugees.* San Remo: International Institute of Human Rights, 1978.

———. *Study of Irregular Movements of Asylum Seekers and Refugees.* Geneva: UNHCR, 1 August 1985.

Keely, Charles B. *Global Refugee Policy: The Case for a Development-Oriented Strategy.* New York: The Population Council, 1981.

Kennedy, David. "International Refugee Protection." *Human Rights Quarterly* 8 (February 1986): 9–69.

Kerll, H. W. "New Dimensions of the Global Refugee Problem and the Need for a Comprehensive Human Rights and Development-Oriented Refugee Policy." in G. S. Goodwin-Gill (ed.). *International Human Rights Law: The New Decade: Refugees Facing Crisis in the 1990s.* Oxford: Oxford University Press, September 1990. 237–51.

Koehn, Peter. *Refugees from Revolution: U.S. Policy and Third World Migration.* Boulder, Colo.: Westview Press, 1991.

Kritz, Mary M. (ed.). *U.S. Immigration and Refugee Policy: Global and Domestic Issues.* Lexington, Mass.: D.C. Heath, 1983.

———, Charles B. Keely, and S. M. Tomasi (eds.). *Global Trends in Migration Theory and Research in International Population Movements.* Staten Island, N.Y.: Center for Migration Studies, 1981.

Kulischer, Eugene M. *Europe on the Move: War and Population Changes, 1917–1947.* New York: Columbia University Press, 1948.

Kuper, Leo. *Genocide: Its Political Uses in the Twentieth Century.* New Haven: Yale University Press, 1981.

Lawyers' Committee for International Human Rights. *The UNHCR at Forty: Refugee Protection at the Crossroads.* New York: Lawyers' Committee for International Human Rights, 1991.

Levy, Deborah M. *Transnational Legal Problems of Refugees: 1982 Michigan Yearbook of International Legal Studies.* New York: Clark Boardman, 1982.

Loescher, Gil. "The European Community and Refugees." *International Affairs* 65 (1989): 617–36.

———. "Humanitarianism and Politics in Central America." *Political Science Quarterly* 103 (Summer 1988): 295–320.

———. "Mass Migration as a Global Security Issue." *World Refugee Survey—1991 in Review* (1991): 7–15.

———, and Bruce Nichols (eds.). *The Moral Nation: Humanitarianism and U.S. Foreign Policy Today.* Notre Dame, Ind.: University of Notre Dame Press, 1989.

Loescher, Gil, and John Scanlan. *Calculated Kindness: Refugees and America's Half-Open Door.* New York: The Free Press and Macmillan, 1986.

——— (eds.). *The Global Refugee Problem: U.S. and World Response.* Special issue of the Annals of the American Academy of Political and Social Science, 467 (1983).

———. *Human Rights, Power Politics, and the International Refugee Regime: The Case of U.S. Treatment of Caribbean Basin Refugees.* Princeton: Princeton University Center for International Studies. World Order Studies Occasional Paper Series, No. 14, 1985.

———. "Human Rights, U.S. Foreign Policy and Haitian Refugees." *Journal of Inter-American Studies and World Affairs* 26 (August 1984): 313–56.

MacAlister-Smith, Peter. *International Humanitarian Assistance: Disaster Relief Organizations in International Law and Organization.* Dordrecht: Martinus Nijhoff, 1985.

Marrus, Michael R. *The Unwanted: European Refugees in the Twentieth Century.* New York: Oxford University Press, 1985.

Martin, David A. "Large-Scale Migrations of Asylum-Seekers." *American Journal of International Law* 76 (1982): 598–609.

——— (ed.). *The New Asylum Seekers: Refugee Law in the 1980's.* Norwell, Mass.: Kluwer Academic Publishers, 1989.

Matas, David. *Closing the Doors: The Failure of Refugee Protection.* Toronto: Summerhill Press, 1989.

McNeill, William, and Ruth Adams. *Human Migrations: Patterns and Policies.* Bloomington: Indiana University Press, 1978.

Melander, Goran. *Refugees in Orbit.* Geneva: International Universities Exchange Fund, 1978.

Meyer, Anne. *Annotated Bibliography on Sanctuary.* (Champaign, Ill.: Urbana Ecumenical Committee on Sanctuary, 1986.

Nafziger, J. A. R. "International Law Bearing on the Entry of Aliens Regardless of Refugee Status." In *The Refugee Problem on Universal, Regional and National Level.* Thessaloniki, Greece: Institute of Public International Law and International Relations of Thessaloniki, 1987. 513–36.

Newland, Kathleen. *Refugees: The New International Politics of Displacement.* Worldwatch Paper 43. Washington, D.C.: Worldwatch Institute, March 1981.

Nichols, Bruce. *The Uneasy Alliance: Religion, Refugee Work, and U.S. Foreign Policy.* New York: Oxford University Press, 1988.

Nickle, James W. "Human Rights and the Rights of Aliens." Working Paper NB-3. College Park: University of Maryland Center for Philosophy and Public Policy. 30 July 1980.

Organization for Economic Cooperation and Development (OECD). *The Future of Migration.* Paris: OECD, 1987.

Paludan, Anne. *The New Refugees in Europe.* Geneva: International Exchange Fund, 1974.

Proudfoot, Malcolm J. *European Refugees, 1930–1952: A Study in Forced Population Movement.* London: Faber and Faber, 1957.

Refugee Documentation Project. *Refugee.* Forum for discussion of Canadian and international refugee issues. Toronto: York University, Refugee Documentation Project. Five times per year.

A Refugee Policy for Europe. London: European Consultation on Refugees and Exiles, 1987.

Refugee Policy Group. *The U.S.-Based Refugee Field: An Organizational Analysis.* Washington, D.C.: Refugee Policy Group, April 1982.

Refugee Studies Program. *Journal of Refugee Studies.* Academic exploration of forced migration and national and international responses. Oxford: Oxford University Press. Quarterly.

Refugees: The Dynamics of Displacement. A Report for the Independent Commission on International Humanitarian Issues [ICHI]. London: Zed Books, 1986.

Report of the International Conference "Refugees in the World: The European Community's Response," The Hague, 7–8 December 1989. Utrecht: Netherlands Institute of Human Rights; Amsterdam: Dutch Refugee Council, 1990.

Rose, Peter I. "The Business of Caring: Refugee Workers and Voluntary Agencies." *Refugee Reports* 4 (1981): 1–6.

———. "The Politics and Morality of U.S. Refugee Policy." *Center Magazine.* September–October 1985, 2–14.

Rubin, Gary. *Refugee Protection: An Analysis and Action Proposal.* Washington, D.C.: U.S. Committee for Refugees, 1983.

Rudge, Philip. "Fortress Europe." *World Refugee Survey 1986 in Review.* New York: U.S. Committee for Refugees, 1987. 5–12.

Rystad, Goran (ed.). *The Uprooted: Forced Migration as an International Problem in the Post-War Era.* Lund, Sweden: Lund University Press, 1990.

Salomon, Kim. *Refugees in the Cold War: Toward a New International Refugee Regime in the Early Postwar Era.* Lund, Sweden: Lund University Press, 1991.

Scanlan, John. "Regulating Refugee Flow: Legal Alternative and Obligation under the Refugee Act of 1980." *Notre Dame Lawyer* 56 (April 1981): 618–46.

———, and G. D. Loescher. "Mass Asylum and Human Rights in American Foreign Policy." *Political Science Quarterly* 97 (Spring 1982): 39–56.

Schechtman, Joseph B. *European Population Transfers, 1939–45.* New York: Oxford University Press, 1946.

———. *Postwar Population Transfers in Europe, 1945–55.* Philadelphia: University of Pennsylvania Press, 1962.

———. *The Refugee in the World: Displacement and Integration.* New York: A.S. Barnes, 1963.

Secretary General's Report on the Root Causes of the Refugee Problem in Africa. Addis Ababa: Organization of African Unity, Secretary General, May 1990.

Segal, A. "Haiti." In A. Segal (ed.). *Population Patterns in the Caribbean.* Lexington, Mass.: D.C. Heath, 1975. 197–204.

Silk, James. *Despite a Generous Spirit: Denying Asylum in the United States.* Washington, D.C.: U.S. Committee for Refugees, 1986.

Simpson, John Hope. *The Refugee Problem.* London: Oxford University Press, 1939.

Sjoberg, Tommie. *The Powers and the Persecuted: The Refugee Problem and the Intergovernmental Committee on Refugees (IGCR), 1938–1947.* Lund, Sweden: Lund University Press, 1991.

Skran, Claudena. *The International Refugee Regime and the Refugee Problem in Interwar Europe*. D. Phil. dissertation, Magdalen College, Oxford, 1989.

Smyser, William R. "Refugees: A Never Ending Story." *Foreign Affairs* 64 (Fall 1985): 154–68.

———. *Refugees: Extended Exile*. New York: Praeger, 1987.

Stein, Barry, and Sylvano Tomasi (eds.). "Refugees Today." *International Migration Review* 15 (Spring–Summer 1981): 331–93.

Stewart, Barbara McDonald. *United States Government Policy on Refugees from Nazism, 1933–1940*. New York: Garland Publishing, 1982.

Stoessinger, John. *The Refugee in the World Community*. Minneapolis: University of Minnesota Press, 1956.

Tabori, Paul. *The Anatomy of Exile*. London: George C. Harrap and Co., 1972.

Takkenberg, A. "Mass Migration of Asylum Seekers and State Responsibility." In *The Refugee Problem on Universal, Regional and National Level*. Thessaloniki, Greece: Institute of Public International Law and International Relations of Thessaloniki, 1987. 787–802.

Teitelbaum, Michael S. "Immigration, Refugees and Foreign Policy." *International Organization* 38 (Summer 1984): 429–50.

———. "Right vs. Right: Immigration and Refugee Policy in the United States." *Foreign Affairs* (Autumn 1980): 21–59.

Tolstoy, Nikolai. *Victims of Yalta*. London: Hodder and Stoughton, 1977.

Tomasi, Lydio F. *In Defense of the Alien*. New York: Center for Migration Studies. Annual since 1983.

——— (ed.). "International Migrations: An Assessment for the 90's." *International Migration Review* 23 (Fall 1989).

Towards Harmonization of Refugee Policies in Europe? A Contribution to the Discussion. Paper for the European Consultation on Refugees and Exiles. Utrecht: Netherlands Institute of Human Rights; Amsterdam: Dutch Refugee Council. October 1988.

Unauthorized Migration: An Economic Development Response. Washington, D.C.: Commission for the Study of International Migration and Cooperative Economic Development, July 1990.

United Nations High Commissioner for Refugees. *Collection of International Instruments Concerning Refugees*. Geneva: UNHCR, 1979.

———. *Handbook of Procedures and Criteria for Determining Refugee Status under the 1951 Convention and the 1967 Protocol Relating to the Status of Refugees*. Geneva: UNHCR, 1979.

———. "Note on International Protection." In *Forty-first Session of the Executive Committee of the High Commissioner's Programme, 1990*. Geneva: United Nations, 27 August 1990.

———. Refugee Documentation Center. *Refugee Abstracts*. Abstracts of international literature on refugees. Geneva: UNHCR, RDC. Quarterly.

———. *Refugees*. Magazine on international refugee situations and issues. Geneva: UNHCR. Monthly.

U.S. Committee for Refugees. *Refugee Reports*. News service on national and international refugee issues. Washington, D.C.: USCR/ACNS. Monthly.

———. *World Refugee Survey*. Washington, D.C.: USCR. Annual.

United States Department of State, Bureau for Refugee Programs. *World Refugee Report*. Washington, D.C.: U.S. Department of State. Annual.

Vernant, Jacques. *The Refugee in the Post-War World*. New Haven: Yale University Press, 1953.

Wasserstein, Bernard. *Britain and the Jews of Britain, 1939–1945.* Oxford: Clarendon Press, 1979.

Weis, Paul. "Human Rights and Refugees." *Israel Yearbook on Human Rights* 1 (1971): 35–50.

———. "The 1967 Protocol Relating to the Status of Refugees and Some Questions of the Law of Treaties." *The British Yearbook of International Law* (1976): 39–70.

Widgren, J. "International Migration and Regional Stability." *International Affairs* 66 (October 1990): 749–66.

Woodbridge, George. *The History of UNRRA.* New York: Columbia University Press, 1950.

World Council of Churches. *Refugees.* Newsletter. Geneva: WCC. Monthly.

Wyman, David S. *The Abandonment of the Jews: America and the Holocaust, 1941–45.* New York: Pantheon, 1985.

———. *Paper Walls: America and the Refugee Crisis, 1938–41.* Amherst: University of Massachusetts Press, 1968.

Zolberg, Aristide. "The Next Waves: Migration Theory for a Changing World." *International Migration Review* 23 (1989): 403–30.

———, Astri Suhrke, and Sergio Aguayo. *Escape From Violence: Globalized Social Conflict and the Refugee Crisis in the Developing World.* New York: Oxford University Press, 1989.

Zucker, Norman L., and Naomi Flink Zucker. *The Guarded Gate: The Reality of American Refugee Policy.* San Diego: Harcourt Brace Jovanovich, 1987.

———. "The Uneasy Troika in U.S. Refugee Policy: Foreign Policy, Pressure Groups, and Resettlement Costs." *Journal of Refugee Studies* 2 (1989): 359–72.

Contributors

GIL LOESCHER is Professor of Government and member of the Kellogg Institute for International Studies at the University of Notre Dame. His most recent publication is *The Politics of Humanitarianism: International Cooperation and the Management of Refugee Problems* (Twentieth Century Fund).

CLAUDIA M. SKRAN is an Assistant Professor of Government at Lawrence University. Since 1987 she has taught courses in refugees, human rights, and world politics. From 1984 to 1986 she was associated with the Refugee Studies Programme at Queen Elizabeth House, Oxford University, where she conducted research on European Refugees in the interwar period.

MARK P. GIBNEY is Associate Professor of Political Science at Purdue University. He is the editor of *Open Borders? Closed Societies?: The Ethical and Political Issues* and is author of numerous academic articles on U.S. human rights and refugee policy.

NORMAN L. ZUCKER and NAOMI FLINK ZUCKER are, respectively, a professor of political science and a lecturer in writing at the University of Rhode Island. Their most recent book is *The Guarded Gate: The Reality of American Refugee Policy*. They have written extensively on American refugee and asylum policy.

JAMES C. HATHAWAY is a professor at the Osgoode Hall Law School of York University, Toronto, where he teaches in the fields of international human rights law and refugee law. He also directs the Refugee Law Research Unit. Most recently he has published a monograph on the origins and interpretations of the Convention refugee definition, *The Law and Refugee Status*.

PHILIP RUDGE has been General Secretary of the European Consultation on Refugees and Exiles, the major consortium of volunteer agencies working throughout Europe on behalf of asylum-seekers and refugees for the past seven years. He has written extensively on the issue of asylum in Europe and on the impact of the European Community of 1992 on refugee and asylum policy.